After spending 12 years in a Catholic seminary, five of which as a professed religious, Dr. Arthur X. Deegan served three years in the US Army and then received a doctorate from the University of Michigan. Then he wrote *The Priest as Manager* and *Developing a Vibrant Parish Council.* He was the first chairman—and later Executive Director of the Conference for Pastoral Development and Council Development, and Executive Director of Cathedral Ministry in the New Millennium. In these positions and as a Bible study group leader for many years, he tries to help individuals and faith-sharing groups to mine new insights into oft-read Scripture passages and see what they never saw before in the word of God. In his retirement, he authored four devotional books.

To my beloved wife who ended her prayers to Jesus, "Your friend, Pat".

Arthur X. Deegan II, PhD

REFLECTIONS BEFORE THE BLESSED SACRAMENT

AUSTIN MACAULEY PUBLISHERS™

LONDON * CAMBRIDGE * NEW YORK * SHARJAH

Ordering Information
Quantity sales: Special discounts are available on quantity purchases by corporations, associations, and others. For details, contact the publisher at the address below.

Publisher's Cataloging-in-Publication data
Deegan II, PhD, Arthur X.
Reflections Before the Blessed Sacrament

ISBN 9798886936773 (Paperback)
ISBN 9798886936797 (ePub e-book)
ISBN 9798886936780 (Audiobook)

Library of Congress Control Number: 2023918674

www.austinmacauley.com/us

First Published 2024
Austin Macauley Publishers LLC
40 Wall Street, 33rd Floor, Suite 3302
New York, NY 10005
USA

mail-usa@austinmacauley.com
+1 (646) 5125767

Table of Contents

How to Use These Pages

Kneeling before Jesus in the tabernacle or exposed on the altar is a magnificent gift of God. Aware of our sinfulness and need for drawing ever closer to Jesus, who did so much for us, we hope to show Him during these few minutes of prayer how much we love Him. However, being human, and despite our intent to focus on Him and nothing else, we often find our mind wandering or distracted only to suddenly realize we forgot where we were and what we wanted to do.

Some spend their time reading favorite prayers. This is good, as long as we remember that prayer is the lifting of mind and heart God, not someone else's thoughts, but ours. We must make those prayers our own.

Similarly, when reading the pages in this book, remember they are meant to be thought starters for you. You must read a little and then meditate on what you have read, asking Jesus to help you make those your own by applying them to your current situation.

One way of trying to maintain our attention solely on Jesus is to use a reflection prepared ahead of time in a devotional book. Such a humble book is this one. In it, you will find a series of reflections to help you to offer yourself more fully every day and especially when you are with Jesus present in the Eucharist. They are homilies given by the author over the years, and last only 3 minutes more or less (except a few times when I got carried away).

Some of the reflections are thoughts that occurred to me as I prayed before the Sacred Host. Others are meditations on words from popes, saints or spiritual writers which I found helpful to me in maintain my focus. Often, they begin with a quotation from Scripture which in itself is deserving of your private meditation before moving on to the reflection itself.

Each reflection has been given a title to indicate the theme of that meditation. They are listed alphabetically in the Table of Contents, with the corresponding page number to assist in finding what you might like.

On a personal note: following the example of St. John as he wrote his first epistle, I can say, "I am writing this so that my joy may be complete." How so? Because it makes me happy to share some of my thoughts before the Blessed Sacrament. Happy because I always have been results oriented, and sharing these thoughts is the completion of part of what I see to be my mission in life. Mother Teresa said, "God is joy. Joy is a sign of union with God—of God's presence. Joy is a sign of generosity. When you are full of joy you share."

Addiction

'**I am the living bread that came down from heaven; whoever eats this bread will live forever; and the bread that I will give is my flesh for the life of the world.**' Words taken from the holy Gospel of St. John. (Jn. 6:51)

At the start of the Co-vid 19 pandemic cartoonists were having a great time drawing pictures of people in stay-at-home situations, overindulging in alcohol, fatty foods, chocolates, ice cream and every conceivable addiction that possessed them. I do not know if satisfying those cravings actually helped people to endure their isolation or not.

What I do know is that I realized how strong is the one addiction I have that some preachers call the only good addiction. I refer to my craving to receive the Holy Eucharist. How spoiled we have become. In normal times, we can be united to Jesus in the Eucharist every day of the week. But when the virus crisis hit, we were denied our daily Bread of Life and had to be content with spiritual communions.

Not to disparage spiritual communions, but I found them becoming for me more and more plaintiff as I sorely missed the real thing. Like a lot of addicts I did not realize how essential to me was my daily fix until I could not get it. Then all I could think of was how can I get it! When will they relax the restrictions? My prayer became less focused on being safe from a disease and more on satisfying my addiction for the Eucharist.

And now that I can once again satisfy this longing for the Bread of Life, I pray that I not take this heavenly banquet so much for granted. I pray that I never again be denied my addiction. I pray that I continue to yearn to fill this craving more and more ardently, that I prize each satisfying union with my Savior as the one worthwhile yearning of my soul. I think I now know how an addiction can possess a person. And this addiction could well be what King David meant in Psalm 42 where he wrote: '**My being thirsts for God, the**

living God.' (Psalms 42:3). I pray that this craving take hold of my thoughts day and night until the next time I can satisfy it.

In a word, I am an addict. And for this I thank the Lord Jesus and his mother Mary.

Advent

'I wonder as I wander out under the sky, How Jesus the Savior did come for to die!' Words taken from a lovely Appalachian Christmas carol.

This season of Advent is a time of preparation: it is a time of penance. For, while we will celebrate the Christmas season with great joy, we have to admit that He is coming only to sacrifice himself for our sins. For this, we are ashamed. We really wish He could have come for some other reason, and so we have a feeling of guilt. We spend these four weeks examining our conscience and confessing our sins. And when we sing "O Come, O come, Emmanuel", we ask Him to come with his mercy.

As we kneel before Jesus, we ask Him to remind us that he is the reason for the season. We ask Him to help us resist the movement to replace the Merry Christmas greeting with the secular Happy Holidays. Not that we would deny the right of others to celebrate Hannukah or Kwanzaa, or any other holiday; we just deny their right to take Christ out of Christmas.

And while our society spends more time thinking about Black Friday and counting the shopping days before Christmas, and while we join in the preparations to give and receive gifts—we pray to do so only in imitation of him who gave us the greatest gift of all: himself on the Cross and here in the Eucharist.

The oft heard refrain in the liturgy of this season, 'Come, Lord Jesus, come' awakens in us a realization of the many ways we ask Jesus to come. At Christmas, yes, we ask him to come as the new born babe in the manger. But we also ask him to come at his second coming with glory and majesty, when we will need his divine mercy. And we ask him to come whenever we present ourselves for Holy Communion. And we ask him to come as we try to see him in the people and events of our everyday life.

As we continue with the season of Advent, let us join in the caroling and the decorating and merry making, but most importantly, let us prepare our soul to be worthy of the many graces he wishes to bring us when he answers our plea: 'Come, Lord Jesus, come!'

Advent Wreath

'The people who walked in darkness have seen a great light;' (Is.9:1).

These words were spoken by Isaiah as part of his long and detailed prophecy about the coming of the Messiah. Each year at this time the biggest thing in the sanctuary after the altar, is this humongous Advent Wreath. We can't help but see it. It must be important, and perhaps worthy of a little explanation. As we watch how each week another candle in it is lit, let us reflect on what it tells us about Jesus who comes to us in the Eucharist and whose coming at Christmas it signifies.

The use of the wreath and candles during Advent is a longstanding Catholic tradition that was originally adopted by Christians in the Middle Ages as part of their spiritual preparation for Christmas.

The wreath and candles are full of symbolism tied to the Christmas season. The wreath itself, which is made of various evergreens, signifies continuous life. The circle of the wreath, which has no beginning or end, symbolizes the eternity of God, the immortality of the soul, and the everlasting life we find in Christ. The pine cones that decorate the wreath symbolize life and resurrection.

Isaiah prophesied the birth of the Messiah.

'The people who walked in darkness
have seen a great light;
Upon those who dwelt in the land of gloom
a light has shone.' (Is.9:1).

This verse has been interpreted as referring to the people of the Old Testament wandering in darkness until a child is born. Isaiah goes on got say,

**'For a child is born to us, a son is given us;
upon his shoulder dominion rests.
They name him Wonder-Counselor, God-Hero,
Father-Forever, Prince of Peace.'** (Is. 9:5)

The wreath then is a visual representation of this historic event. The evergreen branches are dark and confusing, yet ever green with the hope of life. The candles, lit one by one, are first a small glimmer, then increasingly bright, until after all four are lit, they are seen to be the reflection of the strongest one in the center, when the Baby is born and it is lit on Christmas Eve.

Alleluia

As we get older it is only natural that we begin to think more often about the next life and how we will be spending our time then. I used to confound people in our bible study group by saying we will spend eternity singing Alleluia. Here is what St. Augustine wrote about that.

'Our whole activity in heaven will consist of Amen and Alleluia…if any of you now were to stand and say Amen and Alleluia all day long, you would drop with fatigue and boredom; you would drop off to sleep in the middle of your words; you would long to keep quiet. This might make you think an afterlife of this sort would be not at all desirable. You might say to yourself: 'Amen and alleluia—we're going to say that forever and ever? Who will be able to endure it?'

'So let me tell you as best I can. It is not in fleeting sounds that we shall be saying Amen and Alleluia, but with the affection of the mind and heart. After all, what does Amen mean? What does Alleluia mean? Amen—it is true. Alleluia—Praise God. When we will see face to face what we can now see through a mirror, we shall then say with quite a different, an inexpressibly different, feeling of love.'

'We shall be saying Amen with a never satisfied satisfaction, so to speak. Because we will lack nothing, there will be satisfaction; but because it will always be giving delight, that satisfaction will be unsatisfied (or eternal). So that as you will be insatiably satisfied with the truth, you will be saying with insatiable truth, 'Amen—it is true.'

'But who can possibly say what it is like, what *eye has not seen, nor ear heard, nor has it come into the heart of man,* as St. Paul asks us? And so because we shall see the truth with perpetual delight, we shall be fired with love of this truth… and so we shall also praise him with the same kind of voice and say Alleluia. All the citizens of that city will be urging each other to equal heights of praise with the most ardent charity toward one another and toward God. They will be saying Alleluia because they will be saying Amen.'

St. Augustine, the Doctor of Grace, is not the easiest writer to comprehend. But I think that in the presence of Jesus here before us we can ask Him to look forward to this Amen and Alleluia. And we can practice it by saying on our knees: 'Amen, Lord—It is true that you are here flesh and blood, soul and divinity.'

Be Holy as I Am Holy

'Gird up the loins of your mind, live soberly, and set your hopes completely on the grace to be brought to you at the revelation of Jesus Christ. Like obedient children, do not act in compliance with the desires of your former ignorance but, as he who called you is holy, be holy yourselves in every aspect of your conduct, for it is written, 'Be holy because I (am) holy' (cf Lev. Ch. 11).' Words taken from the first letter of St. Peter. (1Pet. 1:13–16)

Jesus' whole purpose in coming among us is to enable us to fulfill the impossible seeming commandment 'Be holy, for I, the Lord, your God, am holy.' We cannot share in the holiness of God simply by wanting to. We can be holy with God's own holiness only by dint of the mystery of water and wine by which we come to share in the divine life of Christ. In other words, only the divine DNA contained in the Sacrament of the altar, contained in the Eucharist, can make us holy as He is holy.

When we receive him into our heart, we become what we receive and thus become able to perform the actions of God: peace, gentleness, mercy, righteousness. These are the life-giving passions of God, which must come to supplant our own destructive passions of jealousy, selfish ambition, greed, belligerence.

We Christians are supposed to be different from those who don't know Christ. We are supposed to function by the same passions that motivate the Heart of Christ. But this is a tall order indeed for our poor human nature, so weak, so hesitant, so fearful. We feel we might crack under the weight of the command to love every day as God loves. And we're not wrong in feeling this way, because we are basically nothing but straw to God's fire. However, no one knows our feebleness better than our creator, and he is just as realistic in providing remedies for our infirmities and fears as we are in finding excuses for our endless hesitations and refusals to love as he loves. And what unheard of remedies he provides!

Especially in his sacred Body and Blood! Oh the healing strength of the immortal food in this Sacrament. By it made one with the incarnate Word, we will surely find all the vitality and joy we need to be holy as he is holy.

The Blind Man

Jesus asked him, 'What do you want me to do for you?' He replied, 'Lord, please let me see.' Words taken from the holy Gospel of St. Luke. (Lk.18:40–41)

And me—what do I want Jesus to do for me? He will do enough if he sustains me from one day to the next. He will fail to reproach me for my cowardice just as soon as I begin to abandon myself to him. Every day he will give me fresh advice, new strength. He will instruct me, encourage me, and will grant that I obtain through his sacrifice all the graces I ask of him.

Like that blind man, I do not see that he is present, I sense it. Like him who cast himself at the feet of the Son of David, and did not doubt that he would touch him even though he did not see him, I abandon myself to the certainty that Jesus is near me, is with me, is inside me when I receive him in the Eucharist. For there, too, I cannot see him, but I know that under the species of bread and wine, he is truly there, nourishing me, fortifying me, even though I scarcely know how to ask it of him.

I am deeply moved when I hold hm in my hands, when I kneel before him in the tabernacle or exposed on the altar. I do not need to see him with my bodily eyes, for I recognize him with the eyes of my faith. Like the blind man who became aware of his presence by the noise of the crowd he attracted where ever he went, I know he is here when I feel the adoration of those about me in this holy place.

What did the blind man then do? He followed his merciful savior, giving glory to God. Like him, I conclude my daily meeting with Jesus by a grateful thanksgiving, glorifying my Savior who by this mystery shares with me his divinity while he humbles himself to permit me to consume his sacred body and blood,

Spiritual writers tell us that the worst pain for the holy souls in Purgatory is a kind of blindness. They are assured a place in heaven, but temporarily they await entry there and are denied the sight of God enjoyed by those inside the pearly gates. Let us pray for them by asking Jesus: Lord, please let them see your Beatific Vision.

Blazing Charity

'I have come to set the earth on fire, and how I wish it were already blazing!' Words taken from the hot Gospel of St. Luke. (Lk.12:49):

Pope Benedict XVI wrote: 'When Jesus talks about fire, he means in the first place his own Passion. Jesus sets fire to the earth. Whoever comes close to Jesus, accordingly, must be prepared to be burned. Being a Christian, then, is daring to entrust oneself to this burning fire.'

Jesus in the tabernacle or exposed on our altar, wishes to enkindle in us the fire of His love, the kind of love that he said he wished to be blazing.

Many of us see the Faith, as we call it, like an insulated, armored, electrified carriage in which we can sit secure behind curtained windows as we hurtle through the dark forests. We don't have to see the frightening forms outside, don't have to see the abysses into which we might drop, don't have to see the poor beggars and forsaken ones crying in the night. We can hurtle along safely into heaven. How different from what Jesus wanted, when he said: **'Do not think that I have come to bring peace upon the earth. I have come to bring not peace but the sword.'** (Mt. 10:34)

In Psalm 29, verse 7 we read: **'The voice of the LORD strikes with fiery flame.'**

It is not by accident that when we look at our monstrance, we seem to see flames of fire emanating from the sacred Host. It is not a calm and sleepy peace that Jesus wishes for us, but a more intimate knowledge of how much on fire he was, and still is, to show a preferential option for the poor and needy. When we can look at him face-to-face before us, and feel the warmth of his love and be consumed by his burning mercy that we will in turn acquire what St. Catherine of Sienna calls the virtue of blazing charity.

We will then join the angel at the third apparition of Mary at Fatima, offering the most precious Body, Blood, Soul and Divinity of Jesus—present on our altar and in all the tabernacles of the world—in preparation for the outrages, sacrileges, and indifference by which He is offended.

Bread of Life

'**The cup of blessing that we bless, is it not a participation in the blood of Christ? The bread that we break, is it not a participation in the body of Christ? Because the loaf of bread is one, we, though many, are one body, for we all partake of the one loaf.**' Words taken from the first letter to the Corinthians. (1Cor. 10:16–17)

For our reflection today, may I offer the following exhortation entitled "Coming to the Bread of Life", from Venerable Thomas a Kempis (+1471), author of *"The Imitation of Christ"*:

'My soul longs for your body, my heart desires to be united with you. Give me yourself—it is enough. But without you there is no consolation. Without you I cannot exist, without your visitation I cannot live. I must often come to you, therefore, and receive the strength of my salvation, lest deprived of this heavenly food, I grow weak on the way. Once, most merciful Jesus, while reaching to the people and healing their many ills, you said, 'I will not send them away fasting, lest they faint in the way.' Deal with me likewise, you who have left yourself in this Sacrament for the consolation of the faithful. You are sweet refreshment to the soul, and he who eats you worthily will be a sharer in, and an heir to, eternal glory.'

'It is indeed necessary for me, who fail and sin so often, who so quickly become lax and weak, to renew, cleanse and inflame myself through frequent prayer, confession and the holy reception of your body, lest perhaps by abstaining too long, I fall away from my holy purpose. For from the days of his youth, the senses of man are prone to evil, and unless divine aid strengthens him, he quickly falls deeper. But Holy Communion removes him from evil and confirms him in good.'

Bread of Life 2

'So they said to him, 'What sign can you do, so that we may see and believe in you? What can you do? Our ancestors ate manna in the desert, as it is written: 'He gave them bread from heaven to eat.' So Jesus said to them, 'Amen, amen, I say to you, it was not Moses who gave the bread from heaven; my Father gives you the true bread from heaven.' Words from the gospel of St. John. (Jn.6:30–32)

As our reflection today I offer from among the many writings of St. Ambrose the following exhortation about the scripture passage you just read.

'It is wonderful that God rained manna on our fathers and they were fed with daily food from heaven. And so it is written: 'Man ate the bread of angels.' Yet those who ate that bread all died in the desert. But the food that you receive, that living bread that came down from heaven, supplies the very substance of eternal life, and whoever will eat it will never die, for it is the body of Christ.'

'Consider now which is more excellent: the bread of angels or the flesh of Christ, which is indeed the body that gives life. The first was manna from heaven; the second is above the heavens. One was of heaven; the other is the Lord of the heavens; one subject to corruption if it was kept until the morrow; the other free from all corruption, for if anyone tastes of it with reverence, he will be incapable of corruption. For our fathers, water flowed from the rock; for you, blood flows from Christ. Water satisfied their thirst for a time; blood cleanses you forever. The Jew drinks and still thirsts, but when you drink you will be incapable of thirst. What happened in symbol is now fulfilled in reality.'

'So the Church, in response to grace so great, exhorts her children, exhorts her neighbors, to hasten to these mysteries, In another passage the Holy Spirit has made clear to you what you are to eat, what you are to drink.' 'Taste,' the prophet says, 'and see that the Lord is good; blessed is the Lord.'

Bread of Life 3

'I am the living bread that came down from heaven; whoever eats this bread will live forever; and the bread that I will give is my flesh for the life of the world.' St. John then goes on to recount how the Jews quarreled among themselves saying, **'How can this man give us (his) flesh to eat?'** Words taken from the holy Gospel of St. John. (Jn. 6:51 and 52)

These listeners treated the word of Jesus as we today treat an April fool's joke. But listen to what St. John Vianney, patron of priests, says about this verse.

If we consider all that God has made, heaven and earth, and that beautiful order that reigns in this vast universe—all manifests an infinite power which has created all things, an admirable wisdom which governs all things, and a supreme goodness which provides for all with the same facility as if it were occupied by one creature alone; all these marvels cannot but fill us with admiration and astonishment.

But if we speak of the adorable sacrament of the Eucharist, we may say that here is the marvel of the love of God for us. Here it is that his power, his grace and his goodness shine in a manner altogether extraordinary. Here is the bread come down from heaven, the bread of angels, which is given us for the food of our souls; here is the bread of strengthening which comforts and sweetens our sorrows, the traveler's bread, the key which opens heaven for us, 'He that receives me,' said the Savior, 'shall have eternal life.' And to give us this bread, Jesus multiplies miracles, turns the world of nature upside down, and suspends all its laws.

Nothing can be compared to the Eucharist. By baptism, it is true, we receive the title of God's children; heaven is opened to us as a consequence, and we are made participators in all the treasures of the church. By reconciliation, the wounds of our soul are healed, and the friendship of God is restored to us. By confirmation, Jesus Christ gives us the spirit of life and power. By the sacrament of the sick, he clothes us with the merits of his death and passion. By holy orders, he communicates to the priest all his powers. By matrimony, he sanctifies our actions, even those in which man seems only to follow natural inclinations. All these are mercies truly worthy a God who is in all things infinite.

But in the Eucharist, he gives us himself; we receive here not only the applications of his precious blood, but the author of grace as well.

Bread of Life 4

'Jesus said to them, 'I am the bread of life; whoever comes to me will never hunger, and whoever believe in me will never thirst. ...I am the living bread that came down from heaven; whoever eats this bread will live forever; and the bread that I will give is my flesh for the life of the world.'' Words taken from the holy Gospel of St. John. (Jn. 6:35,51):

In one week, we celebrate the feast days of 2 of the first 3 American citizens to be canonized. First it is the feast of Saint Elizabeth Ann Seton, the first native born American who was declared a saint in 1975. Then it is Saint John Neuman, a naturalized citizen and the 4th bishop of Philadelphia, canonized in 1977.

The latter was noted for his love of poverty, literally giving up every earthly possession in service to the poor. When Bishop Neumann was asked what his greatest treasure was, he answered, 'The bread of life, which is the Blessed Sacrament.' For our reflection this morning, I offer his prayer before the Holy Eucharist.

'How much I love you, O my Jesus. I wish to love you with my whole heart, yet I do not love you enough. My lack of devotion and my sloth make me anxious. I have one desire, that of being near you in the Blessed Sacrament. You are the sweet bridegroom of my soul. My Jesus, my love, my all, gladly would I endure hunger, thirst, heat and cold to remain always with you in the Blessed Sacrament. Would that in your Eucharistic presence I might unceasingly weep over my sins. Take entire possession of me. To you I consecrate all the powers of my soul and body, my whole being. Would that I could infuse into all hearts a burning love for you. What great glory would be given to you here on earth, if every heart were an altar on which every human will were laid in perfect conformity with your will to be consumed by the fire of your love.'

Bread of Life 5

'I am the bread of life; whoever comes to me will never hunger, and whoever believes in me will never thirst... Whoever eats this bread will live forever.' This is part of the Bread of Life discourse in chapter six of St. John's gospel. (Jn. 6:35, 51)

During Advent we are encouraged to examine where we are on our journey of faith. We should check to see if we might be slipping in some aspect of it, or if we need to prune some extra baggage we might be carrying around. We want to recommit ourselves to deepen our love for our Savior and appreciate more the gifts He has given us. Today, kneeling before in the Eucharist, we might ask if our faith in this mystery is strong enough. Do we accept His teaching? Is our faith unconditional? Do we believe without question that we are eating his flesh and drinking his blood?

Do we truly believe that Jesus and His promises assure us of eternal life? He seemed to warn us by suggesting that without the necessary faith, people would not follow him. And as if to prove what he said, many of those who heard His Eucharistic exhortation did in fact leave him because they lacked faith in him. Without believing in Jesus as the way to everlasting life how could they possibly believe one of the most difficult of all his doctrines, one which cannot be proven by anything visible, our Sacrament of love!

Jesus kept stressing the need for faith. It is still important in our day, that I value this virtue if I am truly to believe in what the priest at Mass proclaims to be the mystery of faith. What is merely visible soon grows common and quickly fails to stir emotion. Any face, any scene, however beautiful, loses its stimulating power over us when we become used to it. In the Eucharist, there is no human face, no human figure. But there is a presence, which obtains all its power of stimulating my soul, all its emotional control of me, from something much better than ordinary sight; namely, my spiritual faith in Jesus.

This is why the Blessed Sacrament never becomes common or usual. There is enough about it that is sensible for our human natural faculties to get a foothold, but the full grasp of it comes from my faith in Jesus. Faith is a supernatural virtue by which we believe a truth above our natural ability to understand on the sole reason that God says it is so. Where else can we find a mystery that is exactly that? In the Eucharist there is only room for pure faith, because we have nothing to go by except the words of God, those memorable sentences that are the essence of the Mass: 'This is my body' and 'This is my blood.' The Eucharist is rightly called "Mysterium Fidei", the Mystery of Faith.

Bread of Life 6

'I am the bread of life.' Words taken from the holy Gospel of St. John (6:35)

The word "bread" ought to mean something to me. It ought to be the keystone of my attitude in receiving Holy Communion. You come to me as food, Lord. If at times I receive you and do not feel nourished more strongly, it is probably because I am trying to make Communion a heroic act of virtue, forcing myself by many tiresome acts. In a word, I work, instead of eating the Bread, rejoicing in your Sacred Heart.

To come to you and tire myself out by too much activity is to miss the whole point of finding rest in you. Not that I should be entirely passive either. I must unite myself to you now within me. But why all the other agitation? One does not go to a banquet to do things, but to eat, to be refreshed. I must stop, then, and taste this heavenly food, this "bread of angels", and remain in contemplation like the angels.

Communion is THE time of affective prayer. If I don't take the time to savor the food in peace, I will leave the banquet table unnourished. I must stop my chattering and allow your sacred Blood to course through my veins. You want to be my strength, so I must stop and feel you energize my every faculty, each of my senses, the depth of my heart. How else will you be able to influence my whole day? You come to me, not to entertain me, or to be entertained by me for 15 or 20 minutes, but to give me strength for the day's battles and duties.

You taught us to pray for our daily bread, meaning all we need for life, to be sure, summed up in this very first need, food. So I must look upon you in the Eucharist as my first need, containing all else. My poor human mind is too small to envisage all virtues and graces at one shot. I can only see things one at a time. You make one grace or gift seem most important, dominate, into which all other graces or gifts are dovetailed. So I should not spend these precious few minutes reciting a menu of petitions, which is focusing on me and my concerns, rather than focusing on You. Only that will give my struggle for perfection an individual character. It simplifies life, connects all my acts, and puts order into the terrible business of spiritual activity. Only that will deepen our personal relationship.

Thus you will give light to my whole interior life, show me my special vocation, give order to my practices of prayer, piety and virtue. You will be the motor of all my actions. You will make my life a patterned continual whole with You in its center.

Bread of Life 7

'I am the bread that came down from heaven.' Words taken from the holy Gospel of St. John. (Jn. 6:41)

Lord Jesus, you are stressing here that you are living. That is, you not only give me life—as the Bread of Life—but you live in the Eucharist Yourself. You come and feed me so I can become holy by practicing the virtues you showed us centuries ago in the gospel. But the gospel is a dead history. My power of understanding these gospel verses is much greater if I can come to grips with your being alive in the Eucharist.

You want me to understand that as the bread come down from heaven, I can visualize all the virtues being lived now by you here on our altar. Of course, you are practicing these virtues in a hidden and invisible way. So, I—as all spiritual writers show us—I must take the pains to see your humility in the Host (by hiding your divinity); your obedience in the Host (by coming at the call of the priest); your patience in the tabernacle (by waiting for our visits)

And so on. But most profitable for me will be to see you practicing the most important virtues: adoration and love of the Father, reparation for sin, thanksgiving and continual recollected prayer.

That is how you spend your time. Not a very active life? On the contrary, that is real living. The kind of life you live yourself and want to impart to me. If I join you in these virtues when you are in my heart, maybe that will be a head start to doing it all day long. That is how I can respond to your command to be holy.

Lord, let me just remember the simple fact that in Holy Communion I have in my heart a friend. Simple courtesy will then demand that I listen to you, that I see you living, being holy. You will not be looking for excuses for my faults, for acts of sorrow, of amendment and so forth. Friends do not visit in order to reproach; so our first minutes together should not be preoccupied with that.

You come in Communion as a familiar. You give here the greatest sign of your love, sweetness, goodness, gentleness, intimacy. The familiarity of a tete-a-test, of a conversation.

Bread of Life 8

'Whoever eats my flesh and drinks my blood remains in me and I in him.'
Words taken from the holy Gospel of St, John. (jn 6:56)

Besides your physical dwelling in me during the few minutes after Communion, Lord Jesus, there is the habitual status if intimacy with you possessed by those who receive you often. It is a question of being "recollected" with you, of turning from the outside to the inside. Recollection, we are told by ascetics, as understood in respect of the spiritual life, means attention to the presence of God in the soul. It means withdrawing from external and earthly affairs in order to attend to God and divine things. It is the same as interior solitude in which the soul is alone with God.

This has very practical consequences. If I am recollected in this way, when I am asked to do something, my first thought is not to see if it is convenient personally, if it is advantageous to me. Rather my first thought is to consult you, Lord Jesus, to know if the thing pleases you, if it will contribute to your glory. My frequent aspiration must be 'Lord, may my very thought, word and deed tend to your greater glory.' If so, that will make me happy. Happy in order to please you. Happy to renounce myself and make a little sacrifice. Happy when love of you becomes a habitual thought; when my heart is sad without you.

How do I get this stage of recollection? By practice. By centering my attention all day long on how you would react in such and such a circumstance. As some used to say a while ago: WWJD (What would Jesus do?). By being God centered and not self-centered.

Once again, I can learn from what Mary did. I remember watching a televised Mass from the Vatican on the feast day of the finding of the child Jesus in the temple. When Pope Francis delivered the homily. he focused on the last words of that gospel account where it said, 'Mary kept all these things in her heart and pondered on them.'

'Keeping and pondering,' the holy Father said. She kept what Jesus said in her mind and pondered on what those words might mean for her. We too must keep in our mind the words of the Gospel when we read it; we must keep in our mind the words of the priest at Mass when he opens the scriptures for us; we must keep in our mind the virtues as we see them practiced when we read the lives of the saints.

And then we ponder on what we keep. We ask what they might mean for us in the here and know—not some day in the future, but as we try to live the present moment.

The Wedding in Cana

'On the third day there was a wedding in Cana in Galilee, and the mother of Jesus was there. Jesus and his disciples were also invited to the wedding. When the wine ran short, the mother of Jesus said to him, 'They have no wine.' (And) Jesus said to her, 'Woman, how does your concern affect me? My hour has not yet come.' His mother said to the servers, 'Do whatever he tells you.' Words taken from the hot Gospel of St. John. (Jn. 2:1–5)

At first sight, this could appear to be an entirely human conversation between a mother and her son, and it is indeed a dialogue rich in humanity. But as we listen to this gospel narrative, Pope Benedict XVI says it is worth going a little deeper, not only to understand Jesus and Mary better, but also to learn from Mary the right way to pray. He tells us that Mary does not really ask something of Jesus. She simply says to him: 'They have no wine.' She does not ask for anything specific, much less that he exercise his power, perform a miracle, produce wine. She simply hands the matter over to Jesus and leaves it to him to decide what to do. In the simple words of Mary, we can see two things: first, her affectionate concern for people, that maternal affection which makes her aware of the problems of others and her maternal readiness to help, in which we trust, which here appears for the first time in Holy Scripture. So to her we entrust our cares, our needs and our troubles.

Second, we see how Mary leaves everything to the Lord's judgment. She had said to the angel Gabriel at Nazareth, 'Let it be done to me according to your word.' This continues to be her fundamental attitude. This is how she teaches us to pray: not by seeking to assert before God our own will and our own desires—however reasonable they might seem to us—but rather by bringing them before him and let him decide what he intends to do or not do, confident that whatever it may be, it will be for our true good.

Sometimes we find it hard to understand Jesus' answer; we don't like it when he calls her, 'Woman.' But this title really expresses Mary's place in salvation history. It points to the future, to the hour of the crucifixion, when Jesus will say to her, 'Woman, behold your son.' 'Woman' also recalls the account of the creation of Eve: in her Adam finds the companion for whom he longed and he calls her, 'Woman.' Here at Cana, then, Mary is the new definitive woman, the companion of our Redeemer, expressing the grandeur of Mary's enduring mission.

We like even less when Jesus asks what this has to do with him. We want to object 'You have a lot to do with her; she bore you in her motherly womb and gave you life by her unconditional Yes to Gabriel.' And when he says his hour has not yet come, we need to understand what this means. Jesus never acts alone and never for the sake only of pleasing others. The Father is always the starting point of his actions; later he will cure only those who first show Faith. Here, because of the trust of his mother, he anticipates his final hour.

Charity

'Again, the kingdom of heaven is like a merchant searching for fine pearls. When he finds a pearl of great price, he goes and sells all that he has and buys it.' Words taken from the holy Gospel of St. Matthew. (Mat. 13:45)

What does a woman do when her husband or finance gives her a beautiful pearl necklace? She shows it off proudly. And what do her friends do? They admire it greatly and praise it to the high heavens.

As we gaze on the greatest pearl of them all in the tabernacle or exposed on our altar, what should we be doing?

Let me summarize what Servant of God Dorothy Day, founder of the Catholic Worker Movement, said about the pearl of great price:

The reason for our existence is to praise God, to love him and serve him, and we can do this only by loving our brothers. 'All men are our brothers.' This is the great truth that makes us realize God. Great crimes, it is true, have been committed in the name of human brotherhood, that may serve to obscure the truth, but we must keep on saying it 'All men are our brothers.' We must keep on saying it because Love is the reason for our existence. It is what we all live for, whether we are the hanger-on in Times Square or the most pious member of a religious community. We are seeking what we think to be the good for us. If we don't know any better, it is because, radio, TV, the press and the pulpit have neglected so to inform us. We love what is presented to us as love, and God is not much presented. It is as hard to see Jesus in the respectable Christian today as in the man on the Bowery. And so the masses have been lost to the church.

We who live in this country cannot be as poor as those who go out to other countries. This is so rich a country that luxury has developed at the expense of necessities, and even the destitute partake of the luxury. We are the richest country of the world, like Dives in the feast in the gospel. We must try hard; we must study to be poor like Lazarus at the gate who was taken into

Abraham's bosom. The gospel doesn't tell us anything about Lazarus' virtues. He just sat there and let the dogs lick his sores. He would be classed by any social worker today as a mental case. But again, poverty, and in his case destitution, like hospitality, is so esteemed by God, it is sometimes to be sought after, worked for, as another pearl of great price.

The Church of the Eucharist

Several of our recent popes have written encyclicals on the Eucharist. Today, please hear some of what Saint Pope John Paul 11 said in his encyclical letter "The Church of the Eucharist", dated Holy Thursday, April, 2003. He wrote:

'We read in the first letter of St. Paul to the Corinthians (1Cor. 11:24 ff) that Jesus offered bread saying: 'Take this, all of you, and eat it: this is my body which will be given up for you.' Then he offered wine and said, 'Take this, all of you and drink from it: this is the cup of my blood, the blood of the new and everlasting covenant…, so that sins may be forgiven.'

'Did the Apostles who took part in the Last Supper understand the meaning of the words spoken by Christ? Perhaps not. Those words would only be fully clear at the end of the *Triduum*, the time from Thursday evening to Sunday morning.'

'The Church was born of the paschal mystery. For this very reason, the Eucharist *stands at the center of the Church's life*. This is already clear from the earliest images of the Church found in the Acts of the Apostles: **'They devoted themselves to the teaching of the apostles and to the communal life, to the breaking of the bread and to the prayers.'** (Acts 2:42). The "breaking of the bread" refers to the Eucharist. Two thousand years later, we continue to relive that primordial image of the Church. At every celebration of the Eucharist, we are spiritually brought back to the paschal Triduum.'

'The Mystery of Faith!' When the priest recites or chants these words, all present acclaim: 'We announce your death, O Lord, and we proclaim your resurrection, until you come in glory.' The thought of this leads us to profound amazement and gratitude. In the paschal event and the Eucharist which makes it present throughout the centuries, there is a truly enormous "capacity" which embraces all of history as the recipient of the grace of our redemption. This amazement should always fill the Church assembled for the celebration of the Eucharist. I would like to rekindle this Eucharistic "amazement"—To contemplate the face of Christ, and to contemplate it with Mary, is the "program" which I have set before the Church.'

'I cannot let this Holy Week pass without halting before the Eucharistic face' of Christ and pointing out with new force to the Church the centrality of the Eucharist. 'From it the Church draws her life. From this "living bread", she draws her nourishment. How could I not feel the need to urge everyone to experience it ever anew? For the Eucharist, as Christ's saving presence in the community of the faithful and its spiritual food, is the most precious possession which the Church can have in her journey through history.'

Civility

'**...Love your enemies, do good to those who hate you, bless those who curse you, pray for those who mistreat you.**' Words taken from the holy Gospel of St. Luke. (Lk. 6:27–28)

I was in a discussion the other day with a couple of friends who were bemoaning the sad state of affairs in our country when polite discourse has given way to rabid denunciation and personal attack on anyone who thinks differently, especially in the world of politics. A visitor from Mars would return to report that divisiveness has become a mark of American life today. How do we change all that? WE don't. At least not alone.

Social scientists tell us that the best way to deepen any relationship is one on one conversation, so we will soon spend some time in conversation with Jesus in the tabernacle or exposed on our altar. What will he say to us?

Jesus, as we visit with him this morning in the Holy Eucharist, will be pleading with us to do what we can to change this polarization. He will remind us that part of being a Christian is to evangelize. That means literally to preach the Good News by word and example, to be the yeast that will leaven our community with the spirit of Jesus and not the standard of the civil world.

As you converse with Jesus this morning, listen to what he tells you:

He reminds us of the gift he has given us in the Eucharist. He gives us the grace to follow in his footsteps. He shows us by his life and death how to live a truly Christian life. His words in the quotation from St. Luke are the pattern for, and the only true measure of, how we are supposed to follow him. '**Love your enemies, do good to those who hate you, bless those who curse you, pray for those who mistreat you.**' (Lk. 6:27–28)

Anyone who carries out these commands in his/her daily life will not participate in the current divisiveness. And others will notice this. They will know we are followers of Christ by our love. They will see the joy which our life brings to others. They will see bridges being built to meet others more than half way. They will be moved to join in fraternal dialogue in seeking an end to the bitterness that only makes life unhappy.

Come to Me

'Come to me, all you who labor and are burdened, and I will give you rest.' Words taken from the holy Gospel of St. Matthew. Mt. 11:28)

Look at Jesus on this altar. Be part of a conversation with Jesus. Hear him say, 'Come…' Jesus seems be talking here about burdensome labor, difficult labor, suffering kind of labor, the kind that you wish to be helped with. And like all pain or problems that we wish to ameliorate, we must first admit that we are in need of help and cannot handle things alone. For Jesus later adds: **'Whoever wishes to come after me must deny himself, take up his cross, and follow me.'** (Mt.16:24)

'Come to me,' says Jesus. 'Take my yoke upon you and learn from me, for I am meek and humble of heart; and you will find rest for yourselves. For my yoke is easy, and my burden light.' (Mt. 11:28–30)

'Come to me,' says Jesus. 'Come to me.' Does not Jesus seem to be calling for help? Just as He said, 'I thirst' from the Cross, indicating he invites us to assuage that thirst by bringing souls closer to him, in the words of Mother Teresa; so his plea to Come is an invitation to help him fulfill his heart's desire, namely to be of service to us by lightening our load. 'Come' he cries out. To ignore this invitation is to refuse to come to his aid. By responding to this invitation, we are helping Him as well as ourselves in carrying our load.

What load? He does not specify. To do so would be to confine and limit. Have no misgivings! Whatever be your suffering, your pain, your burden, it has been foreseen. It is included in His aid. 'Come…and I will refresh you.'

He does not say, 'I will give you directions to find relief; I will send you to some healer somewhere. No!' He says, 'I will refresh you. For the refreshment is Jesus Himself. Feel yourself comforted in the loving arms of this Good Shepherd, of this Divine Messiah. He it is who is our freedom from worry, from all kinds of labor.'

The Communion of Saints

In November, we celebrate the feast of All Saints; and then the feast of All Souls. This would seem to be an appropriate time to reflect, while gazing at Jesus on the altar, or kneeling before him in the tabernacle, on what we mean when we say in the Apostle's Creed that we believe in the Communion of Saints.

Our religion has two dimensions, the personal or individual and the corporate or group. Every one's religion is his own personal affair, and consists essentially of his direct relations with God. So is it with every aspect of our lives. Each one comes into the world alone; each one leaves the world alone. Alone each one has one day to stand before the dread judgment seat. There is something infinitely pathetic about the loneliness of every human soul. But we believe that we reach God, and God reaches us, often and intimately, through the group which is the body of Christ, the church.

The church is a communion of saints; this expression refers first to the holy things (sancta), above all the Eucharist, by which the unity of believers form one body in Christ.

The term refers also to the communion of persons (sancti) in Christ who died for all, so that what each one does or suffers in and for Christ bears fruit for all.

We believe in the communion of Christ's faithful, those who are pilgrims on earth, the dead who are being purified in Purgatory, and those who are blessed in heaven, all together forming one church.

One result off this belief is that we pray to the holy ones in heaven to intercede for us. It can be shown that the Church has always believed, as she believes today, that the saints in heaven hear the prayers of their friends on earth; that, as the Council of Trent teaches us, 'it is good and useful to invoke the saints reigning together with Christ' (Sess. xxv).

The Catholic Church teaches that not all the friends of God are fit immediately after death to see his face and dwell with him eternally. For all God's friends in need, there is a period of purification beyond the grave that we call Purgatory.

A second result of this belief is that these waiting souls can be helped by us on earth. The Council of Trent defined this doctrine, against the denials of Luther and Calvin and their followers. The definition was as follows: 'There is a Purgatory, and the souls there detained are helped by the prayers of the faithful, and principally by the acceptable sacrifice of the altar...' (Sess. vi, cap. 30; Sess. xxii, cap 2–3).

Jesus warned that the sin against the Holy Ghost (final impenitence): **'will not be forgiven, either in this age or in the age to come'** (Matt. 12:32). From which statement of our Lord St. Augustine takes occasion to argue as follows: 'That some sinners are not forgiven either in this world or the next world would not be said with truth, unless there were others who, though not forgiven in this world, are forgiven in the world to come' (*De Civitate Dei*, xxii:24).

To summarize: the word saints comes from the Latin "sanctus" which means holy. There are holy things (sancta) which we hold in common: such as our faith, the sacraments, our charisms, our charity (which is why we say that none of us lives for himself alone).

And there are holy persons (sancti) which together make up the body of Christ —us pilgrims, the suffering souls and the blessed in heaven. Between and among these three, there is a common love for each other which is why we pray to and for each other. Their feast days in November is the reminder the church gives us each year to remind us of what we mean when we pray that we believe in the communion of saints.

Conversation

Kneeling before Jesus exposed on the altar, or in the tabernacle, I invite you to have a private conversation with him. I suggest that the best way to deepen any personal relationship is one on one conversation.

Conversation, according to Webster, is 'An informal spoken exchange of thoughts and feelings; a familiar talk, a close association. The word comes from the Latin *cum* (with) and *versa* (to associate).' Being an exchange makes it not a monologue as most of our prayers seem to be. And being Informal makes it not academic, pre-planned, or a debate about an issue. And Webster also says this exchange includes thoughts/ideas (from the intellect) as well as feelings (from the heart).

One-on-one conversations can influence relationships for the better or for the worse. Some conversations serve only to deepen a negative relationship. Think of the loud mouth; the more you hear him spout off, the more distasteful he becomes. Think of the know-it-all: the more he pontificates, the more resentful you become. Think of the angry maniac: the more he rants and raves, the more you put up defenses.

Other conversations develop a positive relationship. Think of the mentor: the more he shows you the way, the more attached you want to become. Think of the suitor: the more loving his words and action, the more you wish to be possessed. Think of the loving spouse: the more tender he or she becomes, the more affection you return.

So with wishing to form a close association with God: the more you hear and understand his word, the more trusting you become; the more certain you are of his love and protection, the more you feel comforted; the more you feel his guiding hand; the more certain you are in what you do.

The underlying premise of my conversation with Jesus is that I want to deepen my relationship with Him positively. To deepen means TO GROW IN

INTENSITY, TO BE LONG-LASTING. I wish it to be part of my continuing growth in holiness, not an ephemeral "high".

Unless you are privileged to receive a vision, your conversation is mostly <u>your</u> thoughts and words. Still you must pause and try to listen to the inspiration he might send back upon your reflection. That is the source of the feeling of relief or togetherness you often experience after a good confession, a meditative praying of the rosary, a humble reception of the Eucharist, or 20 minutes adoring Jesus on our altar.

Conversation 2

We come here to have a conversation with Jesus in the belief that the best way to deepen any relationship is one on one conversation. Let me explain this.

How many movies or sit-coms have you watched where a despondent GI is devastated by a Dear John letter? It seems that physical separation made the mystery go out of the relationship between the soldier and his girlfriend or spouse. A few years go a friend of mine told me how hard it was to maintain a romance with a girl who lived half way across the country; but it blossomed into marriage when the object of his love moved back to his town. How many stories have you heard about a marriage that failed primarily because the couple stopped communicating with each other? How many hurt feelings were rectified because one or the other person finally had to admit 'Oh, I didn't realize this or that…?'

In human relationships, what begins as an attraction turns into something much more special when the parties reveal the deeper selves to one another. Otherwise, you have what amounts to trying to get blood out of a stone. If I want to grow closer to you, meaning to be more important in your life, I have to open myself to you, share my inner feelings, let you know what I am really like, who I really am. This requires conversation between us. Not the kind of artificial posting of myself that takes place in today's social media, but the spilling of my guts, so to speak, the honest revelation of who I am, warts and all.

The Catechism of the Catholic Church states plainly, 'The Eucharist is "the source and summit of the Christian life" (CCC, 1324). Our worship of Our Eucharistic Lord Jesus—fully and completely present under the consecrated species of bread and wine—continues outside of Mass when the sacred Hosts are reserved in the tabernacle or exposed for veneration, as in an adoration chapel or for a special holy hour.'

Soon to be declared <u>Blessed</u> Fulton J. Sheen wrote: 'The purpose of the holy hour is to encourage a deep personal encounter with Christ. The holy and glorious God is constantly inviting us to hold converse tight him, to ask for such things as we need and to experience what a blessing there is in fellowship with him.'

Of course, I don't mean Jesus is going to talk to you audibly. He visits in silence. God achieves everything, acts in all circumstances, and brings about all our interior transformations. But he does it when we wait for him in recollection and silence. In silence, not in turmoil and noise does God enter into the innermost depths of our being.

God's presence has always been present in us in an absolute silence. And a human being's own silence allows him to enter into a relationship with the Word that is at the bottom of his heart. Man enters into a silence that is God.

Silence is not an absence. On the contrary, it is a manifestation of a presence, the most intense of all presences. The real questions of life are posed in silence. The greatest scientific discoveries are worked out in the quiet of a research lab. Our blood flows through our veins without making any noise; we can hear our heartbeat only in silence.

Man must stand or kneel or sit silently before God and tell him: God, since you gave me a desire for perfection, make me love you more and more. I surrender wordlessly to you, O Lord. I want to be docile and malleable like clay in your hands, for you are a skillful, benevolent potter.

Corpus Christi

'Whoever eats my flesh and drinks my blood remains in me and I in him'
Words taken from the holy Gospel of St. John. (Jn. 6:56)

As I kneel before Jesus, I want to think of one feast we celebrate on a Sunday during the Paschal season, the feast of the Most Holy Body and Blood of Christ, formerly known as Corpus Christi. Why the change in name? Well, the Latin word "corpus" means body; but Jesus talked about His Flesh and Blood. So holy mother Church, agreeing that Jesus is totally present in either or both Species, wants us to think more along the lines of the above quotation from chapter 6 of St. John's gospel, where Jesus spoke of flesh and blood, both of which are present in any body as you well know when you order a steak and specify rare or well done, indicating how much blood you want to come out of the flesh of the meat.

Parenthetically, you will recall how careful our priests were in pointing that out to us during the covid crisis—that if we were omitting the drinking of the chalice, we were still receiving both Body and Blood of Christ in the one Species of bread.

Now back to the quote from St. John. Jesus said that when we eat his Flesh and drink His Blood, we remain IN Him and He IN us. I call your attention to the word "in". He did not say we would be in the same area as he, or across the room from him or even near him. He said we would be IN Him and He IN us. Isn't that what happens when we eat anything? It is in us, becomes part of us, changes out physical make-up. You have heard it said that we become what we eat. This is never more true than with regard to the Eucharist. At every Mass during the Offertory, we hear the priest say, 'By the mystery of this water and wine may we come to share in the divinity of Christ.'

Note also the word "remain". We share in the divinity of Christ not just for a few seconds or the few minutes after the Host is assumed into our human body, but we remain in him and he in us. A couple of verses earlier in the gospel, Jesus said, 'I and the Bread of life …and whoever eats this bread will live forever.' Jesus taught that he is the kingdom of heaven wish is eternal.

Corpus Christi and the Visitation

Each year we celebrate the feast of Corpus Christi, the Body and Blood of Jesus. We also annually celebrate the feast of the Visitation of our Blessed Mother. Reflecting on these two feasts and what they say about each other prompts me to ask myself a few questions.

Mary answered Gabriel, **'Behold, I am the handmaid of the Lord. May it be done to me according to your word.'** (Lk.1:38). She then immediately conceived of the Holy Spirit. From then on, Mary became a different person—she was now the Mother of God. <u>Question</u>: When I have the Eucharist in me, am I different in any way?

Mary became a living tabernacle, bearing the Body and Blood of Jesus in her womb. She then in haste traveled to her cousin Elizabeth to share the good news. She did not hesitate to be the first bearer of Good News even to one who herself was blessed by a special miracle of conception. She would not be bragging about her blessedness but would exultingly share it. <u>Question</u>: When I receive Jesus in the Eucharist and become a living tabernacle, do I hasten to share my good fortune with anyone?

When Elizabeth heard the greeting of Mary, the infant in her womb, St. John the Baptist, leapt for joy, sensing the presence of Jesus. <u>Question</u>: Do I always approach the Eucharist with joy?

Elizabeth asked: 'How does this happen to me that the mother of my Lord should come to me? Blessed are you who believed that what was spoken to you by the Lord would be fulfilled' <u>Question</u>: How strong is my belief that I bear the Son of God in my body when I receive the Eucharist?

Elizabeth wanted to make Mary the important person here, calling attention to her singular favor with God and calling her blessed. But Mary would have none of it, instead giving glory to God. Mary responded in her Magnificat proclaiming the greatness of the Lord by diverting attention away from herself to the Mighty One who has done great things for her. <u>Question</u>:

Do I really appreciate the goodness of the Lord in allowing me to receive his sacred Body and Blood?

Mary remained with Elizabeth about three months, helping to care for her in her pregnancy. <u>Question</u>: Does my reception of the Body and Blood of Jesus prompt me to serve my neighbor?

In a word, Mary's visit to Elizabeth was all wrapped up with her carrying the Body and Blood of a Jesus in her womb. She wanted to share the good news. She wanted to be of service to her cousin. The last thing she was thinking about was herself. Model of humility, she accepted the favor and blessings from God, but understood them to be for the benefit of others and not to focus on her. <u>Question</u>: Do I realize how fortunate I am to be able to receive his Body and Blood, ungrateful sinner that I have been?

There is no closer union of two persons than that of mother and child. Mary and her unborn Child were truly one. Her every living breath was to nourish the growing new life within her. <u>Question</u>: When the Sacred Species remains in my body for ten or fifteen minutes after Communion, do I use that time to deepen my personal relationship with Jesus?

This Eucharist on our altar is Corpus Christi, the sacred Body and Blood of Jesus which Mary first confected in her womb. <u>Question</u>: how often do I say Thank You to Mary for giving me the Body and Blood of Jesus?

Mary of the Visitation was indeed a new person. When we receive the Eucharist, we too become something more than our normal self. St. John Chrysostom says, 'To show the love he has for us he has made it possible for those who desire, not merely to look upon him, but even to touch him and to consume him and to fix their teeth in his flesh and to be commingled with him, in short to fulfill all our love. Let us, then, come back from that table like lions breathing out fire, thus becoming terrifying to the devil, and remaining mindful of the love he has shown for us.'

The Cross

'And just as Moses lifted up the serpent in the desert, so must the Son of Man be lifted up, so that everyone who believes in him may have eternal life.' Words taken from the holy Gospel of St. John. (Jn. 3:14-15)

The season of Lent helps us to never forget the horrible suffering and death of the Lord that was necessary before His glorious resurrection. For our reflection today, permit me to quote Pope Francis:

'The serpent is the sign for sin. We think of the Book of Genesis: it was the serpent that seduced Eve, that suggested that she sin…Christianity…is not a philosophical doctrine, it is not a program of life that enables one to be well formed and to make peace. These are its consequences. Christianity is a person, a person lifted up on the cross. A person who emptied himself to save us. He took on sin. And so just as in the desert sin was lifted up, here God made man was lifted up for us. And all of our sins were there…. One cannot understand Christianity without understanding the profound humiliation of the Son of God, who humbled himself and made himself a servant unto death on the cross.'

'Thanks to the mercy of God, we glory in Christ crucified. And that is why there is no Christianity without the cross, and there is no cross without Jesus Christ. …'

'The heart of God's salvation is his Son who took upon himself our sins, our pride, our self-reliance, our vanity, our desire to be like God. A Christian who is not able to glory in Christ crucified has not understood what it means to be Christian. Our wounds, those which sin leaves in us, are healed only through the Lord's wounds, through the wounds of God made man who humbled himself, who emptied himself…The cross is a mystery, the mystery of the love of God who humbles himself, who empties himself. …'

'Where is your sin? Your sin is there on the cross. Go and look for it there, in the wounds of the Lord, and your sins shall be healed, your wounds shall be healed, your sins shall be forgiven. God's forgiveness is not a matter of canceling a debt we have with him. God forgives us in the wounds of his Son lifted up on the cross.'

Death

'Whoever eats my flesh and drinks my blood has eternal life, and I will raise him on the last day.' Words taken from the holy Gospel of St. John (Jn. 6:54)

November is the month to think of the departed. We pray for and to the dead, with All Saints Day and All Souls Day. But before their after life, they all had to face death. So maybe this is a good day to talk about death and how we think about it. Death fills the good person with joy and consolation. The righteous consider death as the end of their sufferings, their sorrows, their temptations, and all their wants. They consider it the beginning of their salvation. They recall the words of Jesus about eating his flesh and see earthly death as the time for Jesus in the Eucharist to keep his promises.

Listen to what some of the Saints had to say about impending death. When Saint Jerome was told by his friends that he was near death, he gathered all his strength and exclaimed: 'Oh, welcome and delightful message! Come soon, O death! How longingly have I awaited you! Come and deliver me from all the troubles of this world! Come and reunite me with my Redeemer!'

St. John Vianney wrote, 'What inexpressible joy a person experiences who was banished from home or led away into captivity, when told that he or she may return to their own country, to their families and friends! The same happiness awaits a soul which loves God and languishes in the ardent desire of seeing him in heaven in the midst of the saints, who are our real family and friends. Death, my friends, is to the just man what sleep is to the tired laborer who is glad of the approach of night, which will bring him rest after the hardships of the day. Death delivers the just man from the prison of his body.'

The holy king David said, 'Deliver me, my God, deliver my soul from the prison of this body. Who will give me wings like a dove, and I will fly and be at rest?' St. Paul said: 'Unhappy man that I am, who shall deliver me from the body of this death?'

Saint Augustine wrote, 'Oh, how consoling it is to die with your conscience at rest. Tranquility of soul and peace of mind are the most precious gifts we can obtain,' says the Holy Spirit. 'There is no pleasure which is comparable to the joy of an innocent heart.' And again he says, 'The righteous one does not fear death, because by it he is reunited to his Master and put in possession of innumerable delights.'

Death on a Cross

'He humbled himself, becoming obedient to death, even death on a cross.'
Words taken from the letter to the Philippians. (Phil.2:8)

Jesus could have chosen a different way of redeeming mankind, but he chose to do it by crucifixion. The reason is that when satisfaction must be made for some sin, the satisfaction should correspond to the sin. Jesus said, 'If your eye offends, pluck it out; if your hand sins, cut it off.' Or for instance, if one sins by mouth by defaming or swearing, he should seek pardon by mouth from God and neighbor. If through the eyes you have sinned by gazing improperly, proper satisfaction is to weep. If you have sinned by your hands, you should extend them in prayer.

What about the original son against God in the garden of Eden? Adam and Eve listened to the devil and tried to be like God, so Jesus had to humble himself forsaking his divinity and become a man. Our first parents disobeyed the command of their Creator, so Jesus had to become obedient unto death. But why on a cross? Adam and Eve sinned by theft of a forbidden fruit from a tree. Then restitution or reparation should be by returning a fruit to the tree. What fruit? In the hail Marry we say, 'blessed is the fruit of your womb.' Tradition says that the wood of the cross was from the same kind of tree in Eden. Therefore, when Jesus was placed on that tree, the fruit was restored to it.

Just as Adam and Eve's sin brought darkness to the whole human race, so Christ's act of submission to the will of the Father restored light for all of us. Saint Vincent Ferror quotes holy mother Church as saying: 'O God, You decreed that man would be saved through the wood of the cross. The tree of man's defeat became his tree of victory; where life was lost, life has been restored through Christ, our Lord.'

As we kneel or sit before Jesus exposed on our altar, let us thank him for so aptly choosing death on a cross to expiate all our sins.

Elijah

…the angel of the LORD came back a second time, touched him (Elijah), and ordered, 'Get up and eat, else the journey will be too long for you!' (Words taken from the first book of Kings. (1Kings: 19:7)

Elijah has long been recognized as among the greats of the Lord's prophets in the old Testament. Toward the end of his life, he had been warned by Jezebel that the king, would kill him. So Elijah was afraid and fled for his life to Beersheba of Judah. Crossing the desert he became hungry and thirsty and weak and tired and lay down to sleep. That is when an angel brought, I'm a loaf of bread and a jug of water. When Elijah saw this, he ate and drank and went back to sleep. But the angel came again, woke him and said, 'Get up and eat, else the journey will be too long for you.' So Elijah did and found the bread was enough to permit him to continue his mission and eventually turn over his mantle to Elisha before going up to heaven in a chariot of fire.

What does all this have to do with us? It is a prefigure of your life and mine. We may not have been threatened with murder, but we are on a journey, the journey of our life. We acknowledge that we are pilgrims; we are journeying toward a rewarding after-life. Like Elijah we often get tired and weak or even lost as we plow forward through the desert of life's difficulties and temptations.

To each of us Our Lord provides the Bread of angels to give us strength for our journey. He lays before us the Blessed Sacrament and says, 'Take and eat else the journey will be too long for you.' Hopefully He will not have to wake us up repeatedly before we catch on. When we see Jesus lifted on high during the sacrifice of the Mass, we can say, 'My Lord and my all,' for there is nothing more we shall need to finish our journey successfully than the wisdom and courage and self-denial that the Lord offers us as the fruit of eating His bread of life.

As we kneel today before Jesus, let us give thanks for this wonderful bread. Let us resolve to partake of this heavenly Bread often, if not daily, just as we feed our body daily. Let us see this bread as the way to sustain our strength for the journey as Jesus intends it to be. He promises that if we eat his flesh and drink his blood, we will have life everlasting.

Eucharistic Adoration

'Stay with us, for it is nearly evening.' Words taken from the holy Gospel of St. Luke. (Lk. 24:29)

In making these words the title of his Apostolic Letter for the Year of the Eucharist, Pope St. John Paul II gave the Church a clear orientation for our times. More than that, he taught us to pray using these same words. He taught us to pray as the Holy Spirit had taught the two disciples on the road to Emmaus. Poor wayfarers they were: bewildered and dejected men, sorrowing and not quite knowing what to think, not quite knowing what to do.

Another wayfarer came to walk with them on the way. The Pope writes that 'weighed down with sadness, they never imagined that this stranger was none other than their Master risen from the dead. Yet they felt their hearts burning within them (v.32) as he spoke to them and explained the scriptures. The light of the world unlocked the hardness of their hearts and opened their eyes.' (v.31)

It was at this moment that the Holy Spirit caused a mysterious invocation to well up from inside them. They spoke prophetically, not for themselves alone, but for all wayfarers of every time and every place. They spoke for the pilgrim Church, for the Church hungry and thirsty as she makes her way through history. They spoke for the Church, the Bride of Christ, burning with desire to behold his face, to hear his voice, to abide, adoring in his presence: **'Stay with us, Lord.'**

Taking their prayer to heart, Jesus 'went in with them. And it came to pass, whilst he was at table with them their eyes were opened to recognize him; then he vanished out of their sight, but his real presence remained. There, in the Bread set before them on the table, they began with the eyes of faith, to discern the Eucharistic Face of their Lord, the blessed Countenance of Christ hidden beneath the sacramental veil.'

In that moment, after that mysterious Breaking of the Bread, two disciples, with a fire burning in their hearts, discovered with amazement the Eucharistic adoration that, over the course of the centuries, would be discovered and cherished by the Church obedient to the command of her Master,' (v 19)

John Paul's Year of the Eucharist was more than a passing observance: it was a grace of conversion in the strictest sense: a turning toward the Eucharistic Face, a rekindling of that fire that burned in those two disciples. That Eucharistic year was a beginning, not an end. What have we done since? How has it changed us? Live then in the radiance of the Eucharistic Face of Christ.

Evangelization

You will recall the episode in the life of Jesus when he was told that his mother and brothers were waiting outside to see him. He did not go out to see them but said, **'Whoever does the will of my heavenly Father is my bother, and sister, and mother.'** Words taken from the holy Gospel of St. Matthew. (Mt. 12:50)

Jesus was not putting down his mother Mary, when he said his mother was whoever did the will of God. Because of every creature that ever lived, Mary did most excellently the will of God, and thus showed herself to be his mother, spiritually as well as biologically.

A priest asked a young man, 'Why do you spend so much time in prayer?' To which came the answer, 'Because that's the way to gain eternal life.'

Such an answer is a bit myopic. It presupposes that our life is to be centered on obtaining personal sanctification in isolation from the rest of God's wonderful creation. That's just not the way it works.

The Baltimore Catechism had it right. 'Why did God make you? God made me to know him, to love him, to serve him in this world, and to be happy with him forever in heaven.' Note that eternal salvation is listed last. It will come to us only if we do the other things first. The way to gain eternal life is not to focus on self but on serving God, on doing his will.

This broader view gives to the whole Christian life its most admirable character, since it turns us away from making of Christianity a religion of our personal salvation. It is no longer a question of ourselves. It is a question of God relying on us. His life is given over into our hands; he touches us with his light and his grace so that we may be his torch bearers, so that we may communicate his incomparable friendship to all our human brothers and sisters, so that we may stir in their heart the echo of his tenderness and so that, through us, they may perceive his face.

Yes, we must pray as the young man did; but we should do this as a way of recharging our batteries to carry out the will of God. We kneel here before the Blessed Sacrament, asking for the courage to make his message known to others, promising to let his light and love shine through us and thus be seen by all. We recall that the Eucharist is a community sacrament, that we are to share in the divinity of Christ so as to bring his love to others, which was his entire mission, as it must be ours.

Face of God

'Do not hide your face from me; do not repel your servant in anger.' Words taken from Psalm 27, verse 9.

Or from Numbers: **'The LORD bless you and keep you! The LORD let his face shine upon you, and be gracious to you! The LORD look upon you kindly and give you peace!'** (Num 6:24-26)

The phrase "face of God", as used in the Bible, can be easily misunderstood.

The problem begins in the book of Exodus, when the prophet Moses, speaking with God on Mount Sinai, asks God to show Moses his glory. But God warns: '...**But my face you cannot see, for no man sees me and lives.'** (Exodus 33:20)

God then places Moses in a cleft in the rock, covers Moses with his hand until God passes by, then removes his hand so Moses may see only his back.

Did anyone see the face of God and Live? Strangely, Moses thought he did. We read in Exodus (33,11): **'The LORD used to speak to Moses face to face, as one man speaks to another.'** Not to be taken literally. It cannot be, for God does not have a face. Instead, it means that God and Moses shared a deep friendship. Moses saw God with the eyes of his faith.

The patriarch Jacob wrestled throughout the night with 'a man' and managed to survive with an injured hip: So Jacob called the place 'Face of God,' saying, **'Because I have seen God face to face,' he said, 'yet my life has been spared.'** (Gen. 32:31) However, the "man" Jacob wrestled with was probably an angel of the Lord. Jacob saw God with the eyes of his faith.

So why do we pray to see His face?

God is a spirit. God is not human and does not have the features of a human body, such as a face. All of God's prophets observed mental pictures, which were images but not physical human-to-God encounters. We know this because Jesus said about himself "no one has seen the Father except the Son."

The Bible says believers will, indeed, see the face of God, in the New Heaven.

The difference will be that, at this point, the faithful will have died and will be in their resurrection bodies. Knowing <u>how</u> God will make himself visible to Christians will have to wait until that day.

Meanwhile we continue to pray to see God's face. In this biblical language, we are praying for what Moses had: a special friendship with God.

You are thinking: What has this got to do with my kneeling before Jesus on the altar or in the tabernacle? Well, every day at the Communion of the Mass, we have an exposition. When the priest elevates the consecrated bread and wine and says, 'Behold (which means look and see) see with the eyes of your faith, see the face of God who takes away the sins of the world.'

To be sure I get it personally, when I walk humbly down the aisle to the foot of the altar to receive Holy Communion, the priest or the extraordinary minister will elevate the Host and look straight at my eyes and will say "the Body of Christ" which means "see with the eyes of your faith, see the face of Jesus, your personal Savior". And I will say 'Amen' which means I do see it.

In like manner when I put the same consecrated Holst in the monstrance, and then place it lovingly on the altar, my actions are saying to you: 'Behold! Look and see, with the ayes of your faith see the face of Jesus who takes away your sins and mine. I am inviting you to deepen that special friendship that was accorded to Moses and Jacob.'

When I look at Jesus on our altar, I think I am asking for the same thing that Moses and Jacob wanted: a special friendship with God. I look at the sacred host and ask that one day I may see Jesus face to face, not hidden behind the species of bread and wine. I wish to learn a lesson from all these biblical figures who were asking for the same thing. More importantly I trust in Jesus who said the pure of heart will see God. I will see Jesus in his glorified body which Peter, James and John saw on Mount Tabor.

Feeding Us All

'My heart is moved with pity for the crowd, for they have been with me now for three days and have nothing to eat.' Words taken from the holy Gospel of St. Matthew. (Mt. 15:32)

In the Old Testament, when God wanted to feed the Israelites who were starving as they wandered around in the desert, he rained down manna from heaven. The Jewish people had nothing to do with it; they simply gathered up the manna and found it to be food very much to their individual tastes. They had invested nothing in this food and eventually complained about it to Moses.

In St. Mark's recounting of Jesus' feeding the multitude, Jesus wanted to teach an important lesson. He did not on his own provide food for the crowd. He began by asking what food they already had. A few barley loaves and a few fish. Not much for a group of 4000 people. Jesus took their meager contribution, expanded it, multiplied it, made it more perfect, so that they all had their fill. And there were leftovers too!

Jesus is teaching us that we must always bring whatever we have, small as it may be, whomsoever we are, imperfect as we may be, and let him work his miracles with our puny contributions. We must not be ashamed, we must not hold back, we must not be afraid. We must place who we are and what we have in his hands and he will do the rest. He adds, he multiplies, he changes and makes perfect our simple offerings.

At each Mass, Jesus takes a small piece of unleavened bread and a few drops of wine and changes them into the flesh and blood of the Son of God. Talk about multiplying and making perfect! And after Mass he waits patiently in the tabernacle, while we gather and humbly ask him to visit with us for a few minutes. As we sit or kneel before Jesus exposed on our altar or in the tabernacle, we recognize he is doing it again.

God's Creation

'God looked at everything he had made, and he found it very good.' Words taken from thee book of Genesis. (Gen 1:31)

The feeding of the four thousand people with a few loaves of bread and fish looked back and was a reminder to the people of how God fed them with manna from heaven as they wandered through the desert to find their promised land. It also looked forward and was a pre-figure of the Blessed Sacrament with which Jesus would continue to feed His people as we wander through our ordinary lives toward our ultimate fatherland.

When Jesus told the disciples to gather the seven baskets of fragments left over, the ordinariness of those fragments of bread was to remind us that we are not expected to do marvelous things. We are simply to fulfill our daily duties in a spirit of love and obedience to the will of God. St. Theresa, the Little Flower, practiced this to an outstanding way, often referred to as her Little Way. She performed her daily tasks, offering them to Jesus, making sure that they be sanctified out of love for Him. She often asked after completing a task, that her reward would be for Jesus to release a soul from Purgatory. We might do the same thing, offering the ordinary things of our daily life, asking that Jesus would save one unborn baby in danger of abortion.

Jesus was also teaching them and us not to waste any of the blessings he has given to us, starting with the wonderful world he created for us. We learn to respect our world, to try to protect it, and keep it from being disfigured. That is why we are careful to collect recyclables, to keep our property and streets clean, and to refrain from the destruction of the forests.

We speak of God the Father as the creator. We also read in the Bible that the Holy Spirit made order out of chaos at the time of creation. Jesus on this altar, as another person in the Blessed Trinity, gave his life to make amends for mankind's abuse of God's creation, and is telling us we will not benefit from his sacrifice if we do not take care of his creation.

God's Point of View

'Remember, man, that you are dust and unto dust you shall return.'

Words spoken by the priest or minister distributing ashes on Ash Wednesday.

Did you ever find yourself trying to pray to God over and over for something and begin to wonder if it is worth further effort? The lives of the saints and the writings of spiritual directors frequently remind us that we are really not worth very much. We are sinners; we are mortal and worth about only 98 cents in our chemical make-up. How dare I stand before God and have the affront to petition him for anything? He can't pay attention to my little needs when the world is in such a mess. So I meditate on these thoughts and convince myself that I'm a worthless wretch, and I crawl into a hole and stop praying.

On the other hand, we are admonished that while we are dust, we are beloved dust. We are worth much more than sparrows. God knows the number of hairs on my head. Jesus died for me, so he thought I was worth a lot. He told me to come to him and he would make my burden light. So now I try to figure out which point of view is the right one.

Is this just a matter of a pessimistic view versus an optimistic view? Perhaps. But further reflection tells me that it is really a matter of trying to see things from God's point of view. I try to grasp God's perspective on the time-limited, local affairs about which I am praying. I try to think more broadly about life and its vicissitudes. Especially as I grow older, I try to take a longer-range view and position myself for the long run. How different is my point of view from God's.

I begin to see that from God's perspective there is no such thing as a little matter in his big universe. When talking to God, every little thing on my mind takes on a cosmic dimension. There is a Spanish phrase that explains it: 'Cada persona es un mundo—each person is a world.' God cares a lot about the health, happiness, self-worth, suffering, etc. of each single person. At one of his weekly audiences in St. Peter's Square, Pope Francis heard a man shout to him, 'You are one of a kind.' In an instant, the Pope stopped and shouted back, 'But you're one of a kind too.'

From God's perspective, my simple prayers are a delight to the ears of God who has a special personal relationship with me. As we continue our journey through Lent, let us try to adopt always God's perspective on events around us and our reaction to them.

The Goodness of God

'Thus the LORD passed before him and cried out, 'The LORD, the LORD, a merciful and gracious God, slow to anger and rich in kindness and fidelity, continuing his kindness for a thousand generations, and forgiving wickedness and crime and sin; ...' Words taken from the book of Exodus. (Ex 34:6–7a):

When we say, 'So and so is a good person,' what do we mean? Goodness and kindness are among the fruits of the Holy Spirit. Goodness is the giving of oneself—like the sun shines, emits its rays and diffuses its light; like a fire that gives out its warmth, or a spring that pours forth its waters. The sun, the fire, the spring are good because they are fulfilling the purpose of their creation; they exist to give of themselves.

The good person must therefore be the one who gives of self and provides some good for others, and that is what we recognize in calling a person good.

Now Moses was told that the Lord is infinite goodness, the total gift of self, without limits, without reserve either in duration of time or space, or the giving of what He has and is for a thousand generations, that is for all eternity. God is good: eternally, immutably, infinitely. For Him to be is to be good, for God is goodness, kindness, love.

All finite goodness comes from God's infinite goodness, is derived from it, is a tiny rivulet, a mere drop. Our goodness is only what God makes it; it is good only insofar as it is connected with the goodness of God, and it ceases to be when that connection is severed. All these finite examples of goodness attract me: a good meal, a good job, a good relationship. I love them and pursue them and exhaust myself in a pursuit which I know more often than not will come to nothing or be short-lived, leaving me empty and dissatisfied. And all the while I neglect the boundless Good who alone can satisfy me and who is offering himself to me.

The gift of the Eucharist is the most sublime Good I could wish for. Here in the Sacrament of the altar I can accept this Good and let it inspire me to give of myself and practice the virtue of goodness, kindness, love. Unless I am connected to this infinite goodness, my own efforts to be good cannot succeed. I will be like a dead battery that needs to be recharged if it is to turn anything on. My time before the Eucharist, my reception of the Eucharist in Communion, are opportunities to be recharged in imitation of the eternal Goodness.

The Good Shepherd

'When he (Jesus) **disembarked and saw the vast crowd, his heart was moved with pity for them, for they were like sheep without a shepherd; and he began to teach them many things.'** Words taken from the holy Gospel of St. Mark. (Mk. 6:34)

What a poignant scene! This is the 6th chapter of St. Mark. For five chapters, Jesus has been the itinerant preacher. He has been walking from town to town all over Galilee. Crowds have been following him, each person trying to but touch the hem of his cloak to be relieved of their maladies: physical, mental, spiritual. He has had to go aside from the crowds to speak to his Father, and to grab a minute's respite. He has even had to get in a boat and sail away from one side of the lake to the other. And what does he find when he disembarks? Another crowd awaiting his coming to shore. And as Jesus sees them, he knows why they seek him. Because they were like lost sheep.

I've never seen a lost sheep. But I've seen deer caught by the headlights of a car suddenly appearing out of the darkness. And the startled look of the deer which often causes them to freeze and sometimes be run over by an equally startled motorist. I can imagine the look of a lost sheep is somewhat the same. Surprised—lost—unaware—beseeching—unsure—staring vacantly.

I've seen the same look on the faces of the patients on the memory floors of nursing homes when we took Holy Communion to them. Unaware—lost—beseeching—abandoned—staring vacantly.

What is the reaction on the part of Jesus? He doesn't groan and say, 'Not again! Not another mob almost trampling me underfoot!' Hardly. Mark says: when he saw the crowd, Jesus' heart was moved with pity for them. And he proceeded to minister to them tirelessly.

We are not told what Jesus said to them. But we know that his favorite greeting to everyone was 'Peace be with you.' So maybe those were his first words. And if so, then the expression on his face must've been an accompanying smile.

Hidden Life of Jesus and Mary

'Truly with you God is hidden, the God of Israel, the savior!' Words taken from the book of Isaiah. (Is.45:15)

Some of you have read my book on the Blessed Mother which I entitled *The Hidden Life of Mary—From Conception to Coronation.* In it I suggested that the Hidden Life refers not so much to the few years lived by the Holy Family at Nazareth, but to a characteristic which was the fruit of her virtue of humility that permeated every action and event in her life.

The same thing is true for the Second Person of the Blessed Trinity, of whom Isaiah said, 'Truly you are a God of hidden ways.' He was hidden in Mary's womb, hidden in Bethlehem, hidden at Nazareth, hidden in Capharnaum and Galilee, in every place of his public ministry and on Calvary.

His mystical life is also hidden. He lives unseen in the Church. He teaches through her mouth; He gives life through her sacraments; he suffers in her sorrows and triumphs through her victories. The church traverses the centuries, doing good. And as the world did not know him, it does not know His church. Even Christians cannot fathom the hiddenness of Jesus in His church.

Where is Jesus more present than in the Eucharist? Only in heaven is he more present than in the Eucharist. The Blessed Sacrament is a compendium of all His loves. Here is the substance of his mortal life, his body and blood, though we cannot see it. Here are all the treasures of his divine love, also hidden from us. In the Eucharist we touch him, we see him, we share his divinity.

Through baptism he is our possession, our food, our life. He cannot be more present than that, but it is all a mystery to us. When we gaze at the tabernacle, our senses seek in vain for a sign of his sovereign presence. He is hidden there, but we know He is there—silent and hidden as in Mary's womb, motionless as in the sepulcher, immolated as on the cross. As St. Thomas

Aquinas put it: 'Upon the cross only your divinity was hidden, but in the Eucharist your humanity too.'

We will now have about 20 minutes of private adoration and conversation with our hidden Jesus. In your conversation with him, profess your belief in this God of hidden ways. And also please ask him for vocations because without priests we can have no Eucharist.

Holy Communion

'By the mystery of this water and wine may we come to share in the divinity of Christ who humbled himself to share in our humanity.' Words from the Offertory of the Mass:

The Dominican monk, Fra Angelico (beatified by Pope St. John Paul 11, when he named him patron of artists along with St. Luke), painted a series of frescoes in the Dominican priory of San Marco. They adorn the monks' cells, spelling out the life of Christ, one room at a time.

One of these paintings tells of the institution of the Eucharist. It was not the usual representation of Christ's Last Supper, a la Leonardo da Vinci, but rather a meditation on the renewal of the mystery of the Eucharist, such as we enjoy it today. Envision with me this painting: the scene is not the upper room, but in the monastery refectory or dining hall. The Eucharist is presented as the source and summit of religious life, the nourishment and object of all prayerful life. In the detail, the disciple whom Jesus loved (St. John) crosses his hands over his chest in a sign of adoration as Jesus himself places a consecrated wafer on his tongue. Next to him St. Peter folds his hands in an act of Thanksgiving having received the host first. They both are glorying in a direct encounter with the person of Jesus.

Fra Angelico has stripped down the I of this Holy Communion administered by the Lord himself. There is nothing to encourage distraction from the contemplation of the main event. The floor and back wall are bare, painted in earth tones that magnify the simplicity of the mendicant's life. There is no visible source of light that envelops the scene. Bathed in an indwelling light, the colors and figures appear diaphanous. The idealized figures seem already to have taken on their glorified bodies as they are made one with Jesus in the Eucharist. As Michaelangelo once said of Fra Angelico, 'This good monk has visited paradise and has been allowed to choose his models there.'

As we gaze on Jesus, exposed on our altar or in our tabernacle, may we give thanks for this encounter with Our Lord, and ask for an ever-deeper appreciation for sharing in his divinity.

The Holy Souls

'He whom the blessed in heaven see face to face, and whom we adore on the altar in faith, is really the same Jesus.' These are words of the French Carmelite mystic, St. Elizabeth of the Trinity, who died in 1906 and was canonized just a few years ago by Pope Francis in 2016.

St. Elizabeth is another of those pure young women who so loved Jesus and died at a tender age—in her case, age 26. Young Elizabeth had a fiery temper which she seemed to control during her First Communion. Witnesses testified to a profound change in her after Mass. In her own words, she was no longer hungry, 'because God has fed me.'

Later she wrote: 'It seems to me that nothing better expresses the love in God's heart than the Eucharist: it is union, communion, he in us, we in him, and isn't that heaven on earth? Even in faith while awaiting the face-to-face vision we so desire? Then we will be satisfied when his glory appears, when we see him in his light. Don't you find that the thought of this meeting refreshes the soul, this talk with him who loves us so? Then everything disappears and it seems that one is already entering into the mystery of God.'

'I wish to stay always close to him… When we have the Blessed Sacrament exposed on the altar, those are divine hours spent in this little corner of heaven where we possess the vision in substance under the humble Host.'

'The other day someone wrote me such a beautiful thought I want to send it to you: 'Faith is the face-to-face in darkness.' Why wouldn't it be so for us, since God is in us and since he asks only to take possession of us as he took possession of the saints? Only, they are always attentive: They are silent, recollected, and their only activity is to be the being who receives. Let us make a dwelling for him in our soul that is wholly at peace… And may our life be a continual communion, a wholly simple movement toward God.'

The big question is how can this make a difference in my daily life? St. Elizabeth has an answer to that: Her special mission is to help us pass through the difficulties of our time with a certain greatness of soul. In her own words: 'We must be mindful of how God is in us in the most intimate way and go about everything with him. Then life is never banal. Even in ordinary tasks, because you do not live for these things, you will go beyond them.'

The Holy Spirit

In the Pentecost season, we are reminded that the Book of Genesis tells us that when God made heaven and earth out of nothing, when He created the earth and everything in it out of a chaos, when He breathed life into the first man, He did all this by the operation of the Holy Spirit.

When the Father fashioned a Son to dwell in the womb of Our Blessed Mother, He did this by the overshadowing of the Holy Spirit. When Jesus wanted to retool his ragamuffin band of close followers into a stalwart army of teachers and defenders of His truth, he sent the Holy Spirit upon them in the form of tongues of fire. When He gave them the power to forgive sins, He said, **'Receive the holy Spirit.'** (Jn. 20:22)

It was the Holy Spirit who came down and worked all these things which are beyond description and human understanding. And now you might ask: 'How can the bread become the Body of Christ? How can the wine become His most precious Blood?' The answer is obvious: it must be by the working of that same Holy Spirit. Which is why at Mass the priest prays: 'Make holy these gifts, by sending down your Spirit upon them so that they may become for us the Body and Blood of our Lord Jesus Christ.'

Our belief in the Real Presence is rooted, then, in our acceptance of the power of the Holy Spirit to bring about things which surpass nature and cannot be discerned except by faith alone. That same Body and Blood which the Spirit first formed in the womb of a virgin; He now forms under the appearance of bread of wine. That same Spirit, Who is the love of the Father for the Son and the Son for the Father, now makes it possible for us to share in the divinity of Christ by a worthy reception of this great sacrament.

Jesus fed the multitudes in the desert with a few loaves of bread when he realized they were hungry and had no way to acquire food for themselves. That same loving Jesus recognizes our hunger for His love and grace. So He makes it possible for millions of us all over the world to eat His flesh and drink His blood to fulfill our desire, as he explained during the beautiful Bread of Life discourse in St. John's Gospel, chapter 6. We don't need to understand how He can do this. We need only to be grateful that He wants to do it and can do it by the power of His Holy Spirit which He promised to send to us as our daily companion.

Humility

'Take my yoke upon you and learn from me, for I am meek and humble of heart; and you will find rest for yourselves.' Words taken from the holy Gospel of St. Matthew. (Mt. 11:29)

Our word "humility" derives, says St. Thomas Aquinas, from the Latin "humus" or "earth". As applied to humans it means that which is perceived as abject, ignoble, or in everyday language, not worth very much. As a virtue it refers to a person considering his defects and thus having a lowly opinion of oneself, or at least lowering oneself and not putting oneself ahead of others.

The best example of this is Jesus Christ in the Eucharist. Here is God almighty coming down from the Father not just once in human flesh and blood to be sacrificed on the cross, but coming down to us everywhere and any time we call on him to do so. All we see of him is the appearance of bread and wine, because he humbles/lowers himself to hide behind these species.

If we look at his life, we also see the many ways he humbles/lowers himself. He spoke little of himself, always about the Father. He minded his own business, even telling his mother in the temple as a teenager that he must be about his Father's business. He rarely commanded things of people, leaving free will to reign. He accepted name-calling, hostility and even persecution joyfully. He welcomed insults and injuries to the point of a very unfair sentencing to death. He overlooked and forgave the faults of others. He made no come-back when he was slighted, forgotten and disliked. He was kind and gentle even under provocation.

This meekness was not a sign of either stupidity or ineptitude. Because he was God, no-one could really hurt him. He may have seemed to others to be weak, but, to the contrary, it took great strength to let others rule the day. Jesus in the Eucharist is asking us to learn of him, to follow his example in similar circumstances in our daily life.

Hunger for the Eucharist

'O most holy Trinity—Father, Son, and Holy Spirit—I adore thee profoundly. I offer thee the most Precious Body, Blood, Soul and Divinity of Jesus Christ—present in all the tabernacles of the world—in reparation for the outrages, sacrileges and indifference by which he is offended....'
The Angel's Prayer from the third apparition of the Angel at Fatima:

For our reflection today, let me summarize what Fr Ted Dajczer, (+2009) founder of the Families of Nazareth Movement, said about this indifference —

'It is so important that your faith in Christ's love increase and that you believe ever more firmly in his ardent desire to come to you in the Eucharist. When you finally come to believe how greatly he loves you and awaits you, then you will realize that, if you delay, in his folly of love for you, God experiences what psychology calls the torment of looking for someone to come. When you start to believe that Jesus loves you, that in fact he waits for you, then as a consequence of your faith, the hunger for God, the desire for the Eucharist, should awaken within you a painful yearning for his coming.'

The torment of looking for a loved one to come is similar to the torment of love that is rejected. The more a mother loves a child who does not return her love, the greater is her torment in longing to see him again. How much more so if this love is the infinite love of God that you cannot even imagine. How great, then, must His torment be in looking for you to come.

Belief in his desire to meet with you will prevent you from falling into routine behavior, which is one of the greatest threats to your faith. When you come to believe fully in the infinite love of Jesus and when you realize his torment of looking for you to come to the Eucharistic table, then you will no longer be able to live without the Eucharist. The hunger for God and the burning desire to get the Lord will be within you, and routine cannot coexist with that hunger.

The Immaculate Conception

'Hail, holy queen, Mother of Mercy, our life, our sweetness, and our hope!' Words recited after the recitation of the holy rosary.

In December, we celebrate the feast of the patroness of our country, our Blessed Mother under the title of the Immaculate Conception. Scripture does not speak of this. Our catechism says the early Fathers of the Church believed this to be a fact. But serious discussion about it did not begin until about the ninth century when the question of celebrating a day to honor her birth became an issue. For centuries, devotion to Immaculate Mary was kept alive by the piety of devout Catholics who believed in this special gift to Mary. But not by all. Some holy and learned saints, like St. Thomas Aquinas, did not believe in it. He was of the opinion that God rescued Mary within an instant of her conception so that, conceived in sin like all humans, she was born pure of sin. Even St. Bernard of Clairvaux, often called "the bearer of the flame for Mary", was convinced that Mary had to be redeemed like all humans, so she must have had original sin. But he would accept the doctrine if pronounced by a pope.

Then in 1830, as we remind ourselves each Monday when we recite the prayers of the Novena to Mary Immaculate, Mary appeared to St. Catherine Laboure and asked for a medal to be struck showing her image and the words: 'O Mary, conceived without sin, pray for us.' This was done and devotion to Mary Immaculate grew so strong that in just a few short years later, in 1854. belief in the Immaculate Conception became an article of our faith by decree of Pope Pius IX. Then to show that this devotion was for everyone, Mary herself appeared in Lourdes to14 year old St. Bernadette Soubirous in 1858 identifying herself as The Immaculate Conception.

But what about her need to be redeemed? The Catechism of the Catholic Church, quoting a document of Vatican II says, 'The splendor of an entirely unique holiness' by which Mary is 'enriched from the first moment of her conception' comes wholly from Christ; she is 'redeemed, in a more exalted fashion, by reason of the merits of Jesus.'

Intimacy with Christ

'He appointed twelve (whom he also named apostles) that they might be with him and he might send them forth to preach and to have authority to drive out demons.' Words taken from the holy Gospel of St. Mark. (Mk. 3:14-15)

When Jesus chose the twelve Apostles, he revealed the secret of all truthful ministry. Notice that the Apostles' first and foremost duty was simply to be with Him—to spend time in the presence of Jesus, loving him and being loved by him, learning his ways, letting their hearts become more and more aligned with His. Only then were they sent out to preach, heal and deliver others from evil. …Fruitfulness comes from being with him or it will not come at all. Jesus said, 'I am the voice, you are the branches. He who abides in me, and I in him, he it is that bears much fruit, for apart from me you can do nothing.'

How do we grow in intimacy with Jesus? We read his word daily, especially the Gospels. St. Ignatius of Antioch, on his way to martyrdom Rome, wrote a letter in which he said, 'I take refuge in the Gospel as the flesh of Christ.' The gospels are the flesh of Jesus because they allow us to touch him in a very real way—to get to know his ways, his love, his voice. We come to share in his compassion for fallen humanity, and especially for the poor, the sick, and the suffering. We are freed from all kinds of hidden misconceptions about him that we have picked up from a fallen world. On the other hand as St. Jerome warned, 'Ignorance of the scriptures is ignorance of Christ.' How can we be Christ's prophets if we do not know him ourselves.

We also get to know him by spending time with him in prayer, adoring him, thanking him, talking with him about our joys and our struggles. We let him warm us through the rays of his love, through Eucharistic adoration, when we receive him in Holy Communion, when we welcome him into our hearts with hospitality full of reverence and zeal. A curious thing happens as we draw closer to the Lord. Instead of becoming more otherworldly or inward looking, we are propelled outward. The love of Christ compels us because we are convinced that He died for us all. The closer we come to Jesus, the more we are filled with God's unconditional love, and the more we long to give it away to the lost and the broken.

(Based on Mary Healy, professor of sacred scripture.)

It Is Finished

The Last words spoken on the cross were: **'It is finished'** (Jn. 19:30)

If I were to ask you, 'What was the "it" Jesus was referring to? You would probably say something' like 'He was talking about his mission from the Father.' And you would be right. Jesus was born to die on the cross to redeem us. That was his mission, his assignment from the Father.

And what about you and me? Was is our mission? How are we doing in reference to it? Do we need to resolve to do better? At this time of year people are making New Year's resolutions. I remember some years ago my young brother said to me, 'What resolutions are you making? I'll make the same ones and I bet I can keep them longer than you.'

He was always a very competitive person and always wanted to beat me on everything. But he missed the whole point of resolutions. They are not a game, competition. They are supposed to be private and special to each of us for none of us has the same needs to resolve about.

Why is that? Because each of us has our individual mission from God, from our beloved Jesus in the Blessed Sacrament. The concept of New Year's resolutions is just another opportunity to do a little self-examination and resolving to do better. Which takes us to a suggestion about how to make New Year's resolutions. We begin by asking, 'Why did God make me?' One answer I share with everybody is in the Baltimore catechism: 'God made me to know him, to love him, to serve him in this world and to be happy with him forever in heaven.' So what do I need to do better with regard to this fundamental reason for my existence?

But beyond that: what about me as an individual? Did God have some special mission to give to me? Absolutely! Each of us has responsibilities suited to our particular sate of life. It begins with my vocation. Some are called to the married state, while others might be called to a consecrated life, while still others are to tough it out as a single person. Some are given the task of leading, while others are expected to be followers. St. Paul tells us that we all have been given different gifts and are expected to use them; some to teach, some to preach, some to perform menial tasks, some to do great things. Mother Teresa told her nuns: 'Some things I can do better than you and some things you can do better than me, but together we can do great things.' As we kneel here before Jesus, let us ask him to understand the special mission he has given us and to work better at it this year.

Joy

'Joy to the world, the Lord has come; let earth receive her king!'

The words of this popular Christmas carol tell us that Joy is the theme of this holy season. Joy, especially as lived by Jesus himself. As we kneel before Jesus in the Eucharist, let us contemplate the person of Jesus during his earthly life. In his humanity, he experienced our joys. He has known, appreciated and celebrated a whole range of human joys, those simple daily joys within the reach of everyone. Think of all the events in his life when he experienced the joys of daily living.

He admired the birds of heaven and the lilies of the field. He grasped God's attitude toward creation at the dawn of history. He extolled the joy of the sower and the harvester, and the joy of the man who finds a hidden treasure, and the joy of the shepherd who recovers his lost sheep and of the woman who finds her lost coin. He joined in the joy of those invited to the feast, and the joy of the marriage celebration, and the joy of the father who embraced his son returning from a prodigal life. He shared the joy of the woman who had just brought her child into the world.

For Jesus, these joys were real because for him they were the signs of the spiritual joys of the kingdom of God: the joy of the people who enter this kingdom and the joy of the Father who welcomes them there. And for his part, Jesus himself manifested his joy and his tenderness when he met children wishing to approach him, and the rich young man who was faithful and wanted to do more, and friends who opened their home to him, like Mary, Martha and Lazarus. His joy was above all to see the Word accepted, the possessed delivered, a sinful woman or a publican like Zachaeus converted, a woman taking from her poverty and giving a penny. He even exulted with joy when he stated that the little ones have the revelation of the kingdom which remains hidden from the wise and powerful.

Yes, because Christ was a man like us in all things but sin, he accepted and experienced joy as a gift of God. And he did not rest until to the poor he proclaimed the good news of salvation…and to those in sorrow, joy. The miracles of Jesus and his words of pardon are so many signs of God's goodness: all the people rejoiced at all the glorious things that were done by him, and gave glory to God. For us Christians, as for Jesus, it is a question of living the human joys that the Creator gives us day by day as we live in the present. Looking for a practical way to remember? Take a mason jar and resolve each week to put in it a note about a joy you experienced during the week; at year's end you will have a measure of how joyful you have been during the year.

Knowing Jesus

'Getting to know you, getting to know all about you…

Getting to like you, Getting to hope you like me…'

Words taken from a popular Rogers and Hammerstein musical some years ago.

We were made to love and be loved. Especially with regard to Jesus. But how do we get to love someone? I think the popular song got it right: To like someone you have to know that person first. I submit that getting to love Jesus more and more begins by knowing him more and more.

And how do we do that? To know someone, we spend time with him or her. We study that person: his movements, his words, his interactions. We must do the same with Jesus. We spend time with him as we are doing today with him on our altar or when we make a private visit before him in the tabernacle. We study him by reading his life story, the good news of the bible. We watch him by looking at images of him especially representations of him on the cross above our altar and around our necks. We pay attention to what he likes and try to imitate him. We listen to what he asks of us and make a commitment to give what he asks until it hurts.

We hear him say, 'Be holy because I am holy?' 'Is not this what any lover does: try to be more like the beloved? And how do we do that? Recall what Moses said to the people of Israel in the Book of Deuteronomy: 'If you obey the commandments of the Lord, your God…loving him, walking in his ways, and keeping his commandments, statutes and decrees, you will live…and the Lord your God will bless you.'

Jesus himself said: 'You must take up your cross daily and follow me.' Note the little word "daily". Taking up a cross does not means waiting for some terrible sickness or other tragedy and then say, 'I accept this, Lord.' Of course we shroud do this. But the daily crosses are not those major events. They are the little chores, the disappointments, the challenges, the humdrum or monotonous aspects of daily life. To those also we must say, 'I accept these Lord and promise to cope with them by putting my trust in you.'

Let us resolve to know Jesus as a living friend and not only as a historical figure of 2000 years ago. Let us adore him on our altar. Let us look at the crucifix we wear around our neck—really look at it—in order to know, to appreciate him for who he is, the one we want to love more and more.

Lent

We are reminded during Lent that sin is turning our back on God.

Let us reflect on how St. John Eudes (+1680) explains what sin is.

Being the principle, the exemplar, and the end of man and of all creatures, God wishes men to return to him as to their origin, to imitate him, to model their life and their actions on him as their exemplar, to follow him as their rule, to work toward him with all their strength, by every thought, word and action, as to their last end. To render him capable of doing this, God has given man a mind, a heart, and a will to know and love him, to return to him, to imitate him, and to trend unceasingly to him as to his center. And in order that man may do so with joy and facility, God has enlightened his mind with the light of faith, has poured divine grace into his soul, and enkindled love in his heart.

But what has ungrateful man done? He has become separated from God and devoted his interests to self. Instead of employing his love for God, he has devoted it to himself and developed self-love. Instead of returning to God as to his principle, he has turned away from him. Instead of referring to God all the blessings of nature and grace, man appropriates them to himself by complacency and self-esteem, as if they came from himself, who is only nothingness. Instead of following God as his exemplar and his rule, he follows the rule of his passions. Instead of allowing himself to be led by the spirit of God, he desires no other guidance than that of his own inclination. Instead of tending to God as to his end, taking his repose in him and doing everything for him, man wishes to tend wholly to himself and to do everything for self.

Who is God? God is he whose will, interest, pleasure and honor should be performed before every other will, interest, pleasure and honor. What does the sinner do? He prefers his own will, interest, pleasure and honor to the will, interest, pleasure and honor of God. Thus he usurps the place of God, makes a god of self, falls into self-adoration, and pays self the homage that belongs to

God alone. This is the extreme iniquity of sin. This is what we have done every time and as often as we have sinned.

Lent 2

'Sacrifice and offering you do not want;
but ears open to obedience you gave me.
Holocausts and sin offerings you do not require;
so I said Here I am;
your commands for me are written in the scroll.
To do your will is my delight;
my God, your law is in my heart!'
(Words taken from Psalm 40:7–9)

This season of Lent is a time for offering reparations to the Lord for our past infidelities. Homo Sapiens has always felt the need to do penance, as witnessed by the fact that all religions practice some penitential rites.

In the Old Testament, the Mosaic Law as recorded in the book of Leviticus, commanded a cycle of five sacrifices for regular worship: the burnt offering, the grain offering, the sin offering, the guilt offering, and the peace offering. Most of them involved animal sacrifices—goats, sheep and oxen.

To take just one of these, **the burnt offering**—this was the only offering which is to be completely burned—no portion is reserved to be eaten, as was done in the others. The whole sacrifice is turned to smoke so that it becomes a pleasing odor to God, indicating a notion of total surrender to God.

Worth noting is that these sufferings were born by the animals and grain which were put to the torch; not the worshippers who actually had a meal out of it most of the time.

It is also worth noting that the efficacy of these offerings of the people was not lost on dubious rulers of the time. We read for example in the First Book of Kings that Jeroboam, King of Judah, felt 'If this people go up to offer sacrifices in the Temple of the Lord in Jerusalem, the hearts of this people will return to their master.'

In biblical language, we often find the phrase, 'Holocausts and sin offerings' lumped together; this is because all five of the O.T. offerings were burnt on the altar. The sacrifices were liturgical activities.

In the O.T., we also find reference to **sackcloth and ashes** These were worn by someone in mourning to show they had been visited by a disaster. By extension, they were also worn to show remorse in the hopes of appeasing the wrath of God for sins which were a real disaster.

These rites of the O.T. are important to us as descendants of Abraham, but we do not practice them—they have been abrogated by Jesus. In Hebrews (10: 6ff), we are told the Word of God is speaking to the Father. First, he says, 'Sacrifices and offerings, holocausts and sin offerings you neither desired nor took delight in, though they were offered according to the law.' Then he says, 'Behold, I come to do Your will.' He takes away the first to establish the second. By the will of God we have been consecrated through the offering of the body of Jesus Christ once for all. There is no longer any need for these other sacrifices.

As we adore Jesus and look above to the same Jesus on the cross, we take to heart the teaching that only the death of Jesus takes away sin. We are comforted when we hear also the Word of God: **'For I will forgive their evildoing and remember their sins no more.'** (Heb. 8:12)

Today the church recommends that we offer three things as our way of showing we are sorry for our sins: prayer, fasting and alms giving, or works of charity It's not so much giving things up for Lent—it's a matter of doing something positive: raising our minds and hearts to the Lord in prayer, going a little hungry by denying ourselves some normal food intake, and giving of our time and treasure to serve others or to help those less fortunate than we are. Note that the alms we give should not be from what's left over, where it doesn't hurt, but built into our budget. Here I am reminded of something Mother Teresa told her nuns: 'The miracle is not that we give of ourselves for others, the miracle is that we are happy doing so.'

One final note: by any or all of our Lenten practices, we are not buying the forgiveness of God.

Lent 3

During this Lenten season we have been practicing three works of penance: prayer, fasting and alms giving. How to fast is rather clear; and so is the concept of giving alms. But prayer? When are you supposed to do that? How are you supposed to do that? How much praying is enough? Are you ever unsure about what you should pray? Do your prayers become dull or repetitive? How can you know you are praying the way God wants you to?

Perhaps the approach of a craftsman can help. No successful craftsman would approach his work without his tool box, for in it are the tools he needs to ply his trade. You have a prayer tool box. In it are tools to help you have more confidence in your prayers if you use them when you pray.

Do you want to be less distracted and pray more fervently at Mass? Reach into your prayer tool box and take out a missal and follow the Eucharistic prayer and know you are focusing on the message of Jesus himself.

Do you feel motivated to pray more devoutly to the Blessed Virgin? Reach into your prayer tool box and take out a rosary. Using it you will know you are praying the way Mary wants you to, because she has repeatedly told us to pray the rosary.

Are you prompted to honor Mary as the Immaculate Conception? Reach into your prayer tool box and take out a copy of the Miraculous Medal novena which some say continuously.

Do you feel at a loss as to what to say when the priest in the confessional tells you to make a good act of contrition? Reach into your prayer tool box and recall the Act of Contrition you were taught in grade school.

Do you want to pray to be humble when you hear so often at Mass the warning from Jesus that the proud will be humbled and the humble will be exalted? Reach into your prayer tool box and take out a copy of the Litany of Humility and be reminded of numerous ways to be humble in your daily life.

When you are asked to pray to Jesus for vocations, why not reach into your prayer tool box and take out a copy of the Vocations prayer offered by your diocesan vocations office?

Do you have a special intention you want to pray for? Reach into your prayer tool box and take out the Bible. Then take out your cellphone and ask google for bible verses about that issue. You can make those bible prayers your own and have confidence you are praying well because you are using the very words of the Holy Spirit who authored the bible.

Just think about this for a few minutes and you will find all kinds of tools in your prayer tool box just waiting to be put to good use.

Lent 4

We are fast approaching Passiontide. In Holy Week, we will read various gospel versions of the Passion and Death of Our Lord. Have you ever meditated on the differences in the four gospel accounts? Let us recall some of these details as we kneel before Jesus here on our altar. St. Mark emphasizes the *suffering* of Jesus: how he was tragically rejected, unfairly condemned, viciously beaten, horribly insulted, and mistreated by multiple groups. St. Matthew stresses the *kingship* of Jesus, how the de-facto ruling powers (esp. Pilate & Caiphas) conspired to get rid of someone they saw as a political threat. St. Luke gives importance to the *innocence* of Jesus, how Pilate said he did not deserve death, and others (Herod Antipas, the centurion, the repentant thief) also recognized his innocence. While St. John revels in the *exaltation* of Jesus, how he remains in charge, driving all the action, completing the will of the Father, and being glorified as he is lifted up.

One place of stark difference is at the moment of Jesus' death. Matthew has Jesus cry out again the first verse of Psalm 22 **'My God, my God, why have you forsaken me?'** (Mt. 27–46). He might even have yelled out that entire psalm of long-suffering. This is a picture of pure lament, a nightmare imagery: Jesus cries out, people are surrounding him and taunting him. Matthew's Jesus is obedient, a faithful seeker of God's will in his life, obedient to the Torah but questioned by the lament. Then he says Jesus handed over his spirit, which was the Jewish concept of obedient death: you hand back to God the life breath he gave you. Jesus is dying in anguish but still trusting God. This is reflected in what comes next in Matthew's version: the veil of the temple is torn, there are earthquakes, rocks split, tombs open the dry bones of Ezekiel come forth. In St. John's version, there is no cry of abandonment: it is triumphant. Jesus dies saying, 'It is finished.'

Throughout his gospel John uses the word "finish or complete" to summarize Jesus' mission. It is in John's gospel that Jesus forms a new community by speaking to Mary and the beloved disciple from the cross. Only John describes the piercing of the centurion's sword bringing out blood and water, very symbolic of victory to John. Only in John do we read about the breaking of the legs of the two thieves, but leaving the lamb of God untouched. For John death is an exaltation, his circuit back to the Father from whom he had come. Then, too, John's gospel is the most brutal: Jesus is struck when being arrested in the garden; he is interrogated, tortured, pierced so that blood comes out. John does not mask the death. But it is a triumphant, powerful, beautiful triumph over death. Jesus goes to death in majesty.

Lent's Daily Cross

As our Lenten season continues, Jesus from the Cross continues to tell us: **'If anyone wishes to come after me, he must deny himself and take up his cross daily and follow me.'** (Words taken from the holy Gospel of St. Luke. (Lk. 9:23)

In one of his Lenten sermons, Pope Benedict said: There is a key word that recurs frequently in the liturgy to remind us that Jesus is always close to help us carry our crosses; that word is 'daily' understood in its literal sense. Today God reveals his law and we are granted to choose today between good and evil between life or death. Today the kingdom of God is at hand; repent and believe in the gospel. Today Christ dies on Calvary and rises from the dead; he ascends into heaven and is seated at the right hand of the Father; today the Holy Spirit is given to us. Today is a favorable time.'

Pain, sickness, loss of income, strained relationships, trouble of all kinds seem to strike senselessly and often warp the lives of those they touch. Why this person or that one should be given this or that cross to bear is more than any of us can know here and now…What we do know is that God is our Father and he permits only those things to happen to us that are for our good. They are indeed for our own good IF we use them rightly.

'Offer it up' is a stock phrase that will bring a smile of recognition to anyone who has ever gone to a Catholic school. It was a little phrase that in childhood could transform everything from a lost prize or a skinned knee to a dose of bitter medicine or the teasing of a trying companion. With older years and the sophistication of our age, it is easy to forget that life's biggest, sorest, bitterest crosses can be "offered up" in union with our suffering Lord just as successfully as the smaller trials of childhood. Furthermore, they can be endured cheerfully; as coin for heaven. The grace to tale up every cross is expendable, and it is a pity to waste even the tiniest bit. Naturally, this does not mean that a person with a serious illness is expected to fold his hands and die piously without ever calling a doctor. The Lord who gave us remedies expects us to use them. But there will always be crosses which no remedy can cure. What is to be done with that? It is a free gift to us, like the cross thrust on the shoulders of Simon of Cyrene. To grumble while we bear it will not make it any lighter nor relieve us of it…To bear our crosses with regard for him who allows us to carry them is to use wisely and well a sure means to heaven.

Whatever your favorite passion story, let us recall some of these details as we kneel before Jesus here on our altar, repenting for our part in this travesty.

Light of the World

**'The people who walked in darkness
have seen a great light;
Upon those who dwelt in the land of gloom
a light has shone.'**
(Words taken from the book of Isaiah (Isaiah, 9:1)

What is the meaning of this light that shone in the darkness? Saint Paul tells us: **'For the grace of God has appeared, saving all'** (Titus 2:11). But what is this grace? It is divine love, the love that changes lives, that renews history, that liberates from evil, that fills hearts with peace and joy. The love of God is so great that he can become small. He did so by lying in a manger. He does so every day when we receive him in the Holy Eucharist. He does so when we see him exposed on our altar.

We do indeed walk in darkness these days. Whether it is the life taking scourge of a pandemic, or the brutality of the world's terrorists, or the incredulity of government leaders who are like the blind leading the blind—we stumble our way from one futile solution to another. The darkness can sometimes cause us to lose faith.

The latest perversion of the powers of darkness is pinning an undefined label on one's opponent, like calling a pro-lifer an "Idealist". Passing judgement on such a person with words like idealist seems perfectly legitimate, even definitive, the last word on the subject, because these words come from the vocabulary of the esoteric, the elite. That is, until they prove to be vacuous, meaningless, when examined under the light of reason.

But the amazing thing is that the darker a place is, the brighter will be the light; So too with the light of our faith and the grace of God.

We sometimes think that God is good if we are good, as though we can bargain with him to obtain his grace. But that is not how he is. I may have mistaken ideas about all the evils in the world; I may have wandered off the straight and narrow; I may have made a complete mess of things; but the Lord continues to love me. For all my treachery to him, all my lack of faith in him, he continues to love me. His love does not change. It is not fickle; it is faithful; it is patient. God continues to share his abundant love with me, simply because that's the way He is!

So today as we prepare to begin the season Lent, when we shall recall the darkness of the passion and death of Our Savior, let us accompany Him as He marches with head held high toward Calvary's Tree of Life and light, and take comfort in the knowledge that he has shown us the way for he is the Way, the Truth and the Light that shines in the darkness.

Listening

When the Lord called the prophet Samuel as a boy, he was instructed to respond; **'Speak, LORD, for your servant is listening.'** (1Sam. 3:9) I have to admit that my prayer often goes more like, 'Listen, Lord, your servant is speaking.' But prayer is a genuine conversation only if it includes truly listening to the Lord. And the best way to listen to him is through Scripture, his living word.

Scripture is inexhaustible; after reading or hearing the same passage for the hundredth time, the Holy Spirit may reveal something new about it.

'The kingdom of heaven is like a mustard seed that a person took and sowed in a field. It is the smallest of all the seeds, yet when full-grown it is the largest of plants. It becomes a large bush, and the "birds of the sky come and dwell in its branches". (Mt. 13:31–32)

Perhaps you wonder why the kingdom of God so splendid and magnificent, is compared to a tiny mustard seed, and why the consolation of our hope is said to be like such an insignificant thing…I would say that it is a great thing not in its appearance but in its power. For a mustard seed, when one sees it at first, is small, mean and contemptible, not having any taste nor giving off any color, not suggesting any attractiveness. Yet, as soon as it is rubbed, it immediately gives off its odor, manifests its sharpness, breathes out a fiery taste, and is ablaze with such burning heat that it is a cause for wonder that so great a fire should be locked up in these paltry seeds.

So also the Christian faith at first sight seems small, meaning trifling, not big in its power, not giving evidence of a lofty spirit nor proffering grace. Yet when it begins to be rubbed by different temptations, all at once its vigor appears, it manifests its sharpness, breathes forth the warmth of the divine fire that it burns itself and competes whatever partakes of it to burns well. We also are the **"aroma of Christ for God"** as the Blessed Apostle says `. (cf 2Cor 2:15) – Based on Mary Healy, professor of Sacred Scripture

Live Life to the Full

'Not only in extremes,
In moments stark and clear,
In dark night wrestling long and hard
Or agony severe,
But in some faithful act,
Some scarcely conscious choice,
We find the grace to hear and heed
The bidding of Christ's voice.
New crosses wait each day,
New challenges to meet,
New signposts for the way of life,
New marks of death's defeat;
Yet, be they great or small,
Unique or commonplace,
They help us look beyond ourselves
To see and know Christ's face.'

A little poem written by *Fr Jacques Philippe*, a French renowned spiritual director.

Sometimes we get bored with our daily life. It appears humdrum, not very exciting; and we focus on the future, we hope for something more lively or happier. The time when things will go better, circumstances will change, life will be more interesting. At present, we tell ourselves, we don't really have a life, but later we will "live life to the full". Thinking that way we may spend our whole lives waiting to live. Yet, what guarantee is there that we won't be disappointed when the long-awaited time arrives?

Actually, our present life is always something good, for the Creator has endowed it with a blessing he will never cancel, even if we fail to accept the reality of our present lives. God made it, as he made all things, and he saw that it was good.

What we want to do is to live each day of the life God gave us to its full. It doesn't matter whether the job we have at hand is sweeping the kitchen floor or giving a speech to forty thousand people. We must put our hearts into it, simply and calmly and not look for something else to live. Even when what we are doing is genuinely trifling, it's a mistake to rush through it as though we are wasting time. If something, no matter how ordinary, needs to be done and is part of our lives, it's worth doing for its own sake, and worth putting our hearts into.

Living the Eucharist

'For this reason I kneel before the Father…that Christ may dwell in your hearts through faith…so that you may be filled with all the fullness of God.' (Words taken from the letter to the Ephesians. (Eph. 3: 14-19)

Commenting on these words, Pope Francis asked:

How can we come to know Christ? One cannot know the Lord without being in the habit of adoring, of adoring in silence. I believe, if I am not mistaken, that this prayer of adoration is the least known among us; it is the one we engage in the least. Paul immerses himself in the sea which is the person of Christ. And this we can do when we adore Jesus in the Eucharist.

How do we experience the Eucharist? How do we live it? Is it only a moment of celebration, or is it something more? There are very specific signals that tell us if we are living the Eucharist in a good way or not very well. The first indicator is our way of looking at or considering others. In the Eucharist, Christ is always renewing His gift of self. This meant for Him sharing in their aspirations, their problems, Now we, when participating in Holy Mass, find ourselves with all sorts of men and women: young people, the elderly, children; poor and well-off; locals and strangers alike; people with their families and people who are alone. But the Eucharist which I celebrate, does it lead me to truly feel they are all like brothers and sisters? Does it increase my capacity to rejoice with those who are rejoicing and cry with those who are crying? Does it urge me to go out to the poor, the sick, the marginalized? Does it help me to recognize in theirs the face of Jesus?

A second indication, a very important one, is the grace of *feeling forgiven and ready to forgive*. If any one of us does not feel in need of the mercy of God, does not see himself as a sinner, it is better for him not to go to Mass!

We go to Mass because we are sinners and we want to receive God's pardon, to participate in the redemption of Jesus, in His forgiveness. In the bread and in the wine, which we offer and around which we gather, the gift of Christ's body and blood is renewed every time for the remission of our sins.

A last valuable indication comes to us from the relationship between the Eucharistic Celebration and *the life of our Christian communities*. We must always bear in mind that the Eucharist is not something we make; it is not our own commemoration of what Jesus said and did. No. It is precisely an *act of Christ*! It is Christ who acts there, who is on the altar. It is a gift of Christ. Through the Eucharist, Christ wishes to enter into our life and permeate it with His grace, so that in every Christian community there may be coherence between liturgy and life.

Look at the Crucifix

'Behold the Lamb of God who takes away the sins of the world....' (Words from the holy sacrifice of the Mass.)

The priest says these words clearly as he lifts the consecrated Host for our adoration. And what is he asking us to behold? He is obviously referring to the sacrifice of that lamb on the cross, seen on the crucifix nearby. The rubrics of the Mass say that when Mass is offered, there must be a crucifix on the altar or nearby, so we may see the connection between the sacred Host and Jesus on the Cross. For Mass is a re-enactment of the sacrifice of that lamb on that cross, which we call a crucifix.

How many of you are wearing a crucifix around your neck? Everyone? Did you ever reflect on why you wear that crucifix? Hopefully not just because everyone does. Hopefully not just so others can see you are a Catholic. Hopefully not just so you can have a beautiful, glittering piece of jewelry to adorn yourself. Hopefully not just because someone gave it to you at Confirmation or when you got married.

Then let me ask: when was the last time you looked at that crucifix? Really looked at it and meditated on what it means to you? Saints and spiritual writers tell us: Do you want to know how much Jesus loves you? Look at the crucifix! Do you want to know what Jesus expects from you? Look at the crucifix! Do you need to learn to be forgiving? Look at the crucifix! Do you need strength to cope with some problem? Look at the crucifix! Are you wrestling with an important life decision? Look at the crucifix!

The word crucifix means affixed, or attached, to a cross. Who is so affixed? First the Lamb of God. But then each of us, because Jesus said, 'If you do not bear your cross you cannot be my disciple or follower.' Is it any wonder then that we are often given crosses to bear? Each has an opportunity to be like Jesus. Isn't that what it means to be a follower of Jesus?

Unfortunately for most of us we are too busy to look at our crucifix, to really look at it. Why do we not reflect on the meaning of the crucifix often enough? Mother Teresa suggests: 'Once we take our eyes away from ourselves, from our interests, from our own rights, privileges, ambitions—then they will become clear to see Jesus on the crucifix.'

You will say, 'It is hard to look at my crucifix when it is hanging around my neck.' Great! Then _feel_ your crucifix. Feel the outstretched hands thirsting for you. Feel the sacred head surrounded by piercing thorn.

Or take out your rosary and look at the crucifix. Pope St. John Paul 11 in his pastoral letter on the rosary recommends holding its crucifix in one hand while fingering the beads with the other, especially when praying the sorrowful mysteries. My message today: Look at the crucifix!

A Child's Love

'Let the children come to me....' (Words take from the holy Gospel of Mark. (Mk10:14)

You will remember the episode in the life of Jesus. Many people were bringing their children to Jesus so that he might touch them. But his disciples thought they were a bother to Jesus, so they rebuked the parents. Jesus, however, for the only time in all the gospels, became indignant. A pretty strong word, showing his displeasure with his disciples. He insisted: **'Let the children come to me.'**

Why did Jesus say these words? 'Because,' he said, 'the kingdom of God belongs to such as these children.' He then embraced the children, placing his hands on them and blessed them. But he was not done with his followers. He made this a teaching moment by saying, **'Whoever does not accept the kingdom of God like a child will not enter it.'** (Mk.10:15) The message was clear: if we wish to have eternal life with Jesus we must live like children. They must be our model.

How can this be so? Well, just reflect a minute on how children behave. The first thing we all see about them is how they are in awe about everything they see around them in the big people's world... Should this not be our state of mind when we pray, such as before the Blessed Sacrament today?

And when they want something from the necessities of life to toys, they want to play with, what do they do? They plead for them with Mom and Dad. Should this not be our recourse whatever it is we need or desire?

And little ones are always hurting themselves or falling down. What do they do? They come crying to Mom or Dad who will fix their little bruises and help them to get up and try again. Should this not be our approach when needing a cure or going to confession?

And how do they show their love or affection? By throwing themselves in the arms of Mom or Dad with the biggest smile you ever saw. Should this not be the way we approach Jesus and Mary to tell them of our love for them?

So: praising with awe, pleading with confidence and trust, getting up to try once again, or trying to express our love —The children are our model so Jesus can say about us: 'Let them come to me.'

Love the Lord

'For where your treasure is, there also will your heart be.' (Words taken from the holy Gospel of St. Matthew. Mt. 6:21):

St. Alphonsus Mary Liguori was a bishop, Doctor of the Church, and founder of the Congregation of the Most Holy Redeemer, known as the Redemptorists. Here is his prayer before the most holy Eucharist.

'O infinite goodness! O infinite love! A God has given himself wholly to me! Has become all mine! My soul, unite all your affections and draw near to your Lord, who has come expressly to unite himself with you and be loved by you.'

'My dear Redeemer, I embrace you. My treasure! My life! I draw close to you; do not disdain me. Miserable that I am! In the past I have driven you from my soul, and separated myself from you; but for the future I would rather a thousand times lose life than lose you, my sovereign Lord! Forget, Lord, the many times I have offended you, and pardon me. I repent with all my soul. Would that I could die of sorrow. But in spite of all my offenses against you, I feel that you have commanded me to love you.'

'Ah! My Lord! Who am I that you should so desire to be loved by me? But since such is your desire, I wish to please you. You have died for me; have given me your flesh for food in this Eucharist. I leave all, I bid farewell to all, to attach myself to you, my beloved Savior. My dear Redeemer! Whom shall I love if not you, who are infinite beauty and worthy of infinite love? Yes, my God! Where can I find, in heaven or on earth, a greater good than you, or one who has loved me more than you? Ah! Jesus! Take, this morning, possession of my heart; possess it entirely and detach it from all love which is not for you. I choose you alone for my portion, my riches.'

Can you make this prayer yours?

The Love of Jesus

'He loved his own in the world and he loved them to the end.' (Words taken from the holy Gospel of St. John. (Jn13:1)

Who was it that Jesus loved to the end? His end of course was on Calvary. He asked His Father to forgive His executioners because he loved them. He promised the repentant thief that he would be with him in paradise that day because He loved him. He gave His Mother over to the care of St. John, because He loved her. In turn, He gave St. John to the care of His Blessed Mother because He loved him.

And what about us? Jesus said nary a word about us at the end. But actions speak louder than words. He had said many times earlier that He came not to call the righteous, but sinners. And who of us is not a sinner?

Breathing His last, Jesus gave up His spirit and died, telling His Father, 'It is finished.' What was finished? His mission to bring about redemption for all of us by His sacred passion and death, because he loved us all to the end.

All of this is not news to you. In early childhood, you learned this. Growing up, you deepened your understanding of this great love. And kneeling here before the Blessed Sacrament, you continue to meditate on the love Jesus has for you and you in turn have for him, not by reading any book, except the book of your own life.

Jesus gave up everything, including His life, to appear before the Father and sit at His right hand and have a kingdom that will never end. In this same vein, the Little Flower said, 'In the evening of my life I shall appear before you with empty hands. …That gives me joy, for having nothing, I shall receive everything from you.'

That is the lesson of Jesus loving us to the end. All our spiritual wealth, all our supernatural goods, all our life of becoming perfect as our heavenly Father is perfect—all are gone at the end. We shall stand before God empty handed except for the merits of Jesus. In Him, we shall have it all—He shall be ours;

His merits shall be shared with us; His flowing blood shall wash away all of our offenses. We shall be with Him for all eternity, because He loved us to the end.

So learn the lesson of His great love. As Mother Teresa used to say: 'Until you understand the thirst Jesus has for you, you will never understand who he wants you to be, or who He wants to be for you.'

Love the Lord with Your Whole Heart

'You shall love the Lord your God with all your heart, with all your soul, with all your mind, and with all your strength.' (Words taken from the holy Gospel of St. Mark. (Mk. 12:30)

For our reflection today, I offer the following exhortation from Servant of God Archbishop Luis Martinez (+1956), archbishop of Mexico City:

One thing God will not overlook, because he cannot tolerate it—namely, a divided love. He does not wish our heart to be shared between him and creatures, because he desires our whole heart.

One could say that he is satisfied with the heart. It is true that besides the heart, we must give him all our strength, and all our will, because he himself has said so. But with the exception of the heart, he seems to admit delays in all things else, and to bear himself indulgently. Should there be failings in our exterior life, should we have certain faults of character, should we not give him the full fruits of our garden—no matter: our Lord waits. He bears with our weaknesses. But what he will not compound with is our heart; he desires it in its entirety.

And he desires it completely because he loves us, because love is like that: the desire for complete possession is its essential characteristic.

For this reason, our Lord battles unremittingly and at times cruelly—at least so it appears to us—against the inordinate affections of our heart. He is even capable of allowing us to fall into sin in order to cure us of some hidden affection in our heart.

How many times, for instance, in the case of proud souls who are enamored of themselves and consequently deny him the pledged homage of their love, he lets them fall into sin—yes, even mortal sin—when there is no other way whereby to arouse them to a holy humility!

What an awe-inspiring mystery! To think that our Lord would tolerate such a catastrophe to save that poor soul. So that, after having sunk into the mire, it would rise and understand its misery, and then cast away the little idol that it was cherishing in its heart, and at length give itself to him without reserve!'

Loving God

'God made me to know him, to love him, to serve him in this world, and to be happy with him forever in heaven.' (Words from the early Baltimore catechism.)

Let me summarize what Fr Garrigou-Lagrange said about this quotation.

Jesus told us that no-one has seen the Father except the Son; so during our pilgrimage on earth, we must be content with seeing him **"indistinctly, as in a mirror"**, as St. Paul wrote in 1 Corinthians 13:12. It is said that nature is the shadow of God. We are entranced by the reflection of God's perfections, scattered as they are in some small measure among his creatures; we are enchanted by the movement of the planets and stars; we wonder at the beauty of the sensible world; we are amazed at the harmony of colors and sounds, and we are uplifted still more by the splendor of souls as revealed in God's saints.

If we are smart, we will find time to stop and smell the roses from time to time and thank God for this small vision of his glory. I will never forget, as a young seminarian, seeing our 85-year-old Greek professor, sitting in his wheel chair by the garden path, just gazing with complete understanding of the love of God, as he saw a bee pollinating one of his favorite flowers.

But all this is transitory. Paul went on to say, **'At present we see indistinctly, as in a mirror, but then face to face. At present I know partially; then I shall know fully, as I am fully known.'** (1Cor. 13:12) Our true end then, according to revelation, is to know God as he knows himself, to see him face to face as he sees himself, directly and not through creatures. God was in no way obliged to grant us participation in his intimate life, but he could do so and through pure mercy, he decided to do so.

Who will be able to tell the joy that such a vision will produce?

It will produce in us a love of God so strong, so absolute that nothing could ever destroy it or even diminish it. It will produce a love built on admiration, respect and gratitude, but above all on friendship, with the simplicity and familiarity that such a love presupposes. Through such a love we will enjoy above all else that God is God, that he is infinitely holy, infinitely merciful, infinitely just. Everlasting life for us will be to know God as he knows himself, to love him as he loves himself.

Manna Versus the Eucharist

'So they said to him** (Jesus), **'What sign can you do, that we may see and believe in you? What can you do? Our ancestors ate manna in the desert, as it is written: 'He gave them bread from heaven to eat.'** (Words taken from the holy Gospel of St. John. (Jn. 6 :30–31)

You will recall how Jesus, in answer to these unbelievers, contrasted the manna which was the bread of angels to himself as the bread of God. The ancestors who ate the manna all died in the desert. Whereas those who partake of the bread that God gives, who is Jesus, the real Bread, will never be hungry or thirsty.

Jesus is showing the difference between the bread that came down from heaven and the flesh of the Christ who came from above the heavens. One was of heaven; the other is the Lord of the heavens. One would be corrupted if not eaten in one day; the other is free from all corruption, because anyone tasting of it with reverence will be incapable of corruption.

To. complete the contrasting, Jesus reminded them that their ancestors also drank water that came from a rock at the command of Moses, only to complain bitterly that there was not enough to satisfy their thirst. Whereas Jesus is offering his own blood which would make them incapable of thirst. The manna and the water from a rock were a symbol of what is now coming to be in the person of Jesus, the real thing.

So by our devotion to Jesus, exposed on the altar or hidden in the tabernacle, we give thanks, as children of Abraham, that God was generous to the ancestors. But we are very more grateful for his body and blood which can satisfy our hunger and thirst forever.

Martyrs

'These are the ones who have survived the time of great distress; they have washed their robes and made them white in the blood of the Lamb.' (Words taken from the book of Revelation. Rev. (7:14)

Whenever we celebrate the feast of one or more of our Christian martyrs we are reminded by the memory of those ancient and recent heroic witnesses that the Church is Church if she is the Church of martyrs, as his holiness, Pope Francis has said. The ancient history of martyrdom unites with the memory of the new martyrs, of the many Christians killed by the demented ideologies of our own day, killed solely for being disciples of Jesus.

They had the grace to confess Jesus to the end, unto death. They suffered; they gave their life and we received God's blessings through their witness. But there are also many hidden "everyday martyrs"—men and women, faithful to the gentle power of love, to the voice of the Holy Spirit, who in everyday life seek to love God without reservation, and to love their brothers and sisters as themselves.

A martyr can be thought of as a hero, but the fundamental thing about a martyr is that he or she was graced; It is the grace of God, not human courage, that makes martyrs. And 'What does the Church need today?' asks the holy father. Martyrs, witnesses, namely everyday saints. Without them the church can no longer go forth. The Church needs everyday saints, those of ordinary life carried out with coherence; but she also needs those who accept the grace to be witnesses to the end unto death. All those are the living blood of the Church. They are the witnesses who attest that Jesus is risen, that Jesus lives, and affirm it with coherence of life and with the strength of the Holy Spirit which they have been given.

They are the ones who kneel before the Lord on the altar, confess their allegiance to Him, receive Him into their heart as spiritual nourishment and go forth to tell the world what great gift God has given to humankind.

They are the ones who leave the church after Mass to live the parting words of the priest when he says in the name of Jesus: Go now and evangelize the world about you by being an everyday saint.

Mary and the Eucharist

'Before the feast of Passover, Jesus knew that his hour had come to pass from this world to the Father. He loved his own in the world and he loved them to the end....' 'This is my commandment: love one another as I love you. No one has greater love than this, to lay down one's life for one's friends...This I command you: love one another.' (Words taken from the holy Gospel of St. John. (Jn.13:1 and 15:12, 13, 17)

October being a month of special devotion to Our Blessed Mother, I offer for your reflection a summary of a 2007 exhortation of Pope Benedict XVI entitled "*The Sacrament of Love*" in which he spoke of Mary and the Eucharist.

'From the Annunciation to Pentecost, obedient faith in response to God's work shapes Mary's life at every moment. A virgin attentive to God's word, she loves in complete harmony with his will; she treasures in her heart the words that come to her from God, and piecing them together like a mosaic, she learns to understand them more deeply (cf. Luke 2:19, 51). Mary is the great believer who places herself confidently in God's hands, abandoning herself to his will. This mystery deepens as she becomes completely involved in the redemptive mission of Jesus. In the words of the Second Vatican Council, 'the Blessed Virgin advanced in her pilgrimage of faith, and faithfully persevered in her union with her Son until she stood at the Cross, in keeping with the divine plan (cf Jn 19:25), suffering deeply with her only-begotten Son, associating herself with his sacrifice in her mother's heart, and lovingly consenting to the immolation of the victim who was born of her. From the Annunciation to the Cross, Mary is the one who received the Word, made flesh within her and then silenced in death. It is she, lastly, who took into her arms the lifeless body of the one who truly loved his own "to the end" (Jn 13:1).'

'Consequently, every time we approach the Body and Blood of Christ in the eucharistic liturgy, we also turn to her who, by her complete fidelity, received Christ's sacrifice for the whole Church. The synod fathers rightly declared that 'Mary inaugurated the Church's participation in the sacrifice of the Redeemer.' She is the Immaculata, who receives God's gift unconditionally and is thus associated with his work of salvation. Mary of Nazareth, icon of the nascent Church, is the model for each of us, called to receive the gift that Jesus makes of himself in the Eucharist.'

Mary and the Eucharist 2

In the 6th and final chapter of his encyclical *The Church of the Eucharist*, Pope St. John Paul II explained the place of Mary in the Eucharistic Church.

The connection between Mary and the Eucharist is the bond between mother and son. It is a profound relationship. 'Mary is present,' the Pope says, 'with the Church and as the Mother of the Church at each of our celebrations of the Eucharist. If the Church and the Eucharist are inseparably united, the same ought to be said of Mary and the Eucharist.' The holy Father proposes Mary as our teacher in how to contemplate the Eucharist by developing three dispositions: obedience in the faith, sharing in his passion and the spirituality of the *Magnificat*.'

First and foremost an invitation to Jesus' **obedience in the faith**, If the Eucharist is a mystery of faith which so greatly transcends our understanding as to call for sheer abandonment to the word of God, then there can be no one like Mary to act as our support and guide in acquiring this disposition.

A second Eucharistic disposition that Mary teaches us is that of **sacrifice**. From her offering of Jesus in the temple until calvary, Mary lives a type of anticipated spiritual communion of desire and offering that will have its fulfillment in her union with her Son in his passion as well as in the post Easter Eucharistic celebrations presided over by the Apostles...Receiving the Eucharist, Mary receives Jesus anew in her womb, reliving with him the sacrifice of the cross, inviting us to do the same.

A third disposition that Mary teaches us is that of the **spirituality of the *Magnificat*,** since the Eucharist is a canticle of praise and thanksgiving. 'In the Eucharist, the Church is completely united to Christ and his sacrifice, and makes her own the spirit of Mary.' In her canticle, Mary announces the wonder that surpasses all others, the redemptive Incarnation.

Devoting an entire chapter to the presence of Mary in the Church that celebrates the Eucharist, the Holy Father is not doing anything other than explaining what he had stated quite succinctly in his Marian encyclical regarding the Blessed Virgin's spiritual motherhood. 'Her motherhood is particularly noted and experienced by the Christian people at the Sacred Banquet—the liturgical celebration of the mystery of the Redemption—at which Christ, his true body born of the virgin Mary, becomes present. The piety of the Christian people has always very rightly sensed a profound link between devotion to the Blessed Virgin and worship of the Eucharist. 'Mary guides the faithful to the Eucharist.' No wonder John Paul threw himself at the feet of Mary with his motto "Totus Tuus", totally yours.'

Mary and the Eucharist 3

As we behold the Resurrected Flesh of Jesus on our altar in this, the month dedicated to Mary, let us reflect on what one of the Monte Corona hermits wrote about the relationship between the body of Jesus and his blessed Mother.

Mary is the true Mother of God; she conceived him by the operation of the Holy Spirit; she formed his body with her blood; she clothed God with her own flesh. She bore him nine months in her most pure womb; she brought him forth without stain of her virginal purity; she nursed and brought him up, and he was subject to her, he obeyed her, loved her, and honored her, his true mother. She may well say to the God made man, 'Your flesh is my flesh, your blood is my blood; I gave it to you when I conceived you, when I nursed you.'

'The flesh of Jesus,' says Saint Augustine, 'is the flesh of Mary; and although it was exalted by the glory of the Resurrection, it still remained the same as he had received from Mary. With reason was it said by Denis, the Carthusian, that, after the hypostatic union, there is none so close as that of God with his mother. Wherefore Saint Peter Damian had no difficulty to say that Christ was one and the same thing with Mary.'

This is a nobility that surpasses all human and angelic thought; nobility joined to such dignity, that it exceeds all greater highness which can be said or imagined after God; a dignity so exalted, so sublime that it is a supreme union with an infinite Person. 'Next to the being of God,' says Saint Albertus Magnus, 'comes that of the mother of God and she could not be more united to God without becoming God and she alone has limited the omnipotence of God, who can make a greater heaven, a greater earth, a greater world, but cannot make a greater being than the Mother of God.'

So let us today worship this body and blood of Jesus for his greater glory and to honor his mother whose exaltation is greater than all except her humility at being given such favor.

Mary Our Mediatrix

'We have but one Mediator, as we know from the words of the Apostle, 'For there is one God, and one Mediator between God and men, himself a man, Christ Jesus, who gave himself a ransom for all' (1 Tim 2:5–6) … By her maternal charity, Mary cares for the brethren of her Son who still journey on earth surrounded by dangers and difficulties, until they are led to their happy fatherland. Therefore, the Blessed Virgin is invoked by the Church under the titles of Advocate, Auxiliatrix, Adjutrix, and Mediatrix. These, however, are to be so understood that they neither take away nor add anything to the dignity and efficacy of Christ the one Mediator.' (Words from the Dogmatic Constitution on the Church, Vatican Council II (#60,62)

Years before Vatican II St. Louis Grignon de Monfort (+1716) had much to say, urging devotion to our Blessed Mother.

Our Lord is our Advocate and Mediator of redemption with God the Father. It is through him that we must pray with the whole Church, triumphant and militant. It is through him that we have access to God the Father. We should never appear before God, our Father, unless we are supported by the merits of his Son, and, so to speak, clothed in them, as young Jacob was clothed in the skin of the young goats when he appeared before his father Isaac to receive his blessing.

But have we no need at all of a mediator with the Mediator himself? Are we pure enough to be united directly to Christ without any help? Is Jesus not God, equal in every way to the Father? Therefore, is he not the Holy of Holies, having a right to the same respect as his Father? If in his infinite love he became our security and our Mediator with his Father, whom he wished to appease in order to redeem us from our debts, should we on that account show him less respect and have less regard for the majesty and holiness of his person?

Let us not be afraid to say with Saint Bernard that we need a mediator with the Mediator himself and the divine-honored Mary is the one most able to fulfill this office of love. Through her Jesus came to us. Through her we should go to him. If we are afraid of going directly to Jesus, who is God, because of his infinite greatness, or our lowliness, or our sins, let us implore without fear the help and intercession of Mary, our Mother. She is kind; she is tender; and there is nothing harsh or forbidding about her, nothing too sublime or too brilliant.

Mary's Dignity

The divine maternity is the foundation, source, and root of all Mary's graces and privileges, both those that preceded it, as preparation, and those that accompanied it or followed from it, as its consequence. It was by way of preparation for the divine maternity that Mary was the Immaculate Conception, preserved from the stain of original sin by the future merits of her Son. He redeemed her as perfectly as was possible; not by healing her, but by preserving her from the original stain before it touched her soul for even an instant. It was because of her maternity that Mary received the initial fulness of grace which ceased not to increase till it reached its consummated plenitude. And because of the same maternity she was exempt from all personal fault, even venial, and from all imperfection, for she never failed in promptitude to obey the divine inspiration. ...The dignity of Mary surpasses therefore that of all the saints combined.

Recall, too, that Mary had a mother's authority over the Word of God made flesh...The Word made flesh was subject to Mary in most profound sentiments of respect and love. How, then, could we fail to have the same sentiments in regard to the Mother of our God?

In one of the most beautiful books written about Mary, the *Treatise on True Devotion to the Blessed Virgin*, Saint Louis de Montfort says: 'God made man found liberty in being enclosed in her womb; he showed his power by allowing himself to be carried by her, young maiden though she was; he found glory, and his Farther found glory too, in hiding his splendor from all creatures on earth, so as to reveal them to Mary alone; he glorified his majesty and his independence by depending on the virgin in his conception, his birth, his presentation in the temple, his hidden life of thirty years—and even up to the time of his death, for she was present then, and he offered one only sacrifice in union with her, and was immolated to the eternal Father with her consent, as once Isaac was immolated to the divine will by the consent of Abraham. It is she who nourished and supported him, who brought him up and then sacrificed him for us. Finally, Our Lord remains as much the Son of Mary in heaven as he was on earth.'

Mary, Undoer of Knots

August is the month of the Immaculate Heart of Mary. This month is full of devotion to our Blessed Mother; we have the dedication of St. Mary Major; throughout the month we have many saints known for their devotion to Mary: St. Dominic, St. Maximilian Kolbe, St. Bernard, St. Monica among others. And we have the two powerful feasts: the Assumption and the Queenship of Mary.

As we look at our Lord exposed on the altar, I'd like to mention a devotion to the mother of Jesus being made popular by Pope Francis; namely, Mary, the Undoer or Untier of Knots. While studying in Germany in the 1980s, he discovered this devotion at the Church of St. Peter in Augsburg. In the church, there is a painting from about 1700 that depicts Mary in heaven surrounded by angels. She stands on the crescent moon crushing the head of the serpent, Satan. She holds a long ribbon and is untying a large knot, one of several on the ribbon.

The inspiration for this devotion came from St. Irenaeus in the second century writing about Mary, the second Eve. The first Eve was disobedient and was the cause of death for herself and for the whole human race. Mary on the other hand was obedient as the handmaid of the Lord; Thus the knot of Eve's disobedience was undone or untied by the obedience of Mary.

This devotion had a profound impact on the devotional life of Pope Francis. As archbishop of Buenos Aires, he introduced and encouraged the devotion to Our Lady, Undoer of Knots. The devotion was so intensely popular throughout Argentina and Brazil that the British Guardian called it 'a religious craze.'

Such a devotion to Mary could be a big help in our First Friday devotion to Jesus in the Eucharist. How? Month after month we kneel before Jesus and promise to undo the knots that plague our lives. There are two kinds of knots. Often the "knots" of life are of our own making. How often we "knot-up" our own life by disobeying the commandments and the teachings of the church, and then even blame God and others (as did Adam and Eve) for what we chose to do. Nevertheless, with humble and contrite hearts, we can depend upon the prayers and intercession of our Blessed Mother to show us the way and to help us unknot our lives so as to live up to the promises we make to Jesus. Second—Sometimes our lives may seem one big knot due to circumstances beyond our control, as when we face a serious medical problem, financial failings or difficulties in relationships.

There is a special prayer to Our Lady, Undoer of Knots. This beautiful prayer, similar to the "Memorare", moves us to invoke the compassion of our Blessed Mother. It says, for instance: 'Virgin Mary, mother of Jesus and my mother, cast your compassionate eyes upon me and see the snarl of knots that exist in my life. You know very well how desperate I am, my pain, and how I am bound by these knots. O Powerful Mother, by your grace and intercessory power with your Son and my liberator, take into your hands today the knots of my life. Undo them for the glory of God.'

So today we pray: Our Lady Undoer of Knots, pray for me.

Mercy

'Happy those whose help is Jacob's God,
whose hope is in the Lord, their God,
The maker of heaven and earth,
the seas and all that is in them,
Who keeps faith forever,
secures justice for the oppressed,
gives food to the hungry...'
(Words taken from Psalm 146 (Ps 146:5–7)

These are signs of God's mercy. In short, the mercy of God is not an abstract idea, but a concrete reality through which he reveals his love as that of a father or a mother. In the parables devoted to mercy, Jesus reveals the nature of God as that of a father who never gives up until he has forgiven the wrong and overcome rejection with mercy.

At the start of our recent Jubilee Year of Mercy, our Holy Father explained Mercy: 'We need constantly to contemplate the mystery of mercy. It is a wellspring of serenity, joy and peace. Our salvation depends on it. Mercy: the ultimate and supreme act by which God comes to meet us.'

The mission Jesus received from the Father was that of revealing the mystery of divine love in its fullness. 'God is love,' St. John affirms for the first and only time in Holy Scripture. This is the path which the merciful love of Christians must also travel. Just as he is merciful, so we are called to be merciful to each other. The church's very credibility is seen as how she shows merciful and compassionate love.

Followers of Christ may reflect on the corporal and spiritual works of mercy. It will be a way to reawaken our conscience. Let us enter more deeply into the heart of the Gospel where the poor have a special experience of God's mercy. Jesus introduces us to those works so we will know we are living as his disciples. The <u>corporal</u> signs of mercy: Feed the hungry, give drink to the thirsty, clothe the naked, welcome the stranger, heal the sick, visit the imprisoned and bury the dead. The <u>spiritual</u> signs of mercy: counsel the doubtful, instruct the ignorant, admonish sinners, comfort the afflicted, forgive offenses, bear patiently those who do us ill, pray for the living and the dead. May the sweetness of her countenance watch over us so that all of us may rediscover the joy of God's tenderness.

Mercy 2

'I am convinced that the whole church will find in this jubilee year the joy to rediscover and render fruitful the mercy of God, with which we are all called to give consolation to every man and woman of our time.'

(Words from the encyclical of Pope Francis when he announced the Jubilee year of Mercy:

As we gaze up on the merciful Jesus in the Eucharist, have we truly considered the message about mercy, which the holy father called "the beating heart of the Gospel"? Have we determined to live a life of mercy not for just one year but for always?

Listen to what Venerable Archbishop Fulton J Sheen said about mercy:

'Mercy, Our Lord reminded us, is something more than a sentimental, emotional, tender-heartedness. The very word mercy is derived from the Latin *miserum cor*, a sorrowful heart. Mercy is therefore a compassionate understanding of another's unhappiness.'

A person is merciful when he feels the sorrow and misery of another as if it were his own. Disliking misery and unhappiness, the merciful person seeks to dispel the misery of his neighbor just as much as he would if the misery were his own. That is why, whenever mercy is confronted not only with pain, but with sin and wrongdoing, it becomes forgiveness which not merely pardons, but ever rebuilds into justice, repentance and love. Mercy is a compassion that seeks to unburden the sorrows of others as if they were our own. But if we have no such compassion, then how can compassion ever come back to us?

Unless we throw something up, nothing will come down; unless there is an action, there can never be a reaction; unless we give, it shall not be given to us; unless we love, we shall not be loved; unless we pardon evil, our evil shall not be forgiven; unless we are merciful to others, God cannot be merciful to us. If our heart is filled with the sand of our ego, how can God oil it with the fire of his Sacred Heart? If there is no "for sale" sign on the selfishness of our souls, how can God take possession of them?

If then, we wish to receive mercy, we must think of others, for it seems that God finds us best when we are lost in others.

Mercy 3

'While he (the son) **was still a long way off, his father caught sight of him, and was filled with compassion. He ran to his son, embraced him and kissed him.' (**Words taken from the holy Gospel of St. Luke. (Lk. 15:20)

In the parables devoted to mercy—the lost sheep, the lost coin, the prodigal son—Jesus revels the nature of God as that of a father who never gives up until he has forgiven the wrong with compassion and mercy.

Pope Francis stated in his official announcement of the Extraordinary Jubilee Year of Mercy, that he would like us to place the Sacrament of Reconciliation and adoration of the Blessed Sacrament at the center of our lives. The Church of mercy seems to be the hallmark of Francis' papacy. Over and over again Pope Francis emphasizes the primacy of mercy as the foundation of how our Church projects the love of God and His beloved Son plentifully evident in the gospels. The father of the prodigal son does not demand that the son on his return fall on his knees pleading for mercy and forgiveness, but joyfully embraces him and calls for a feast.

Jesus in the Eucharist is our Bread of Life, food for sinners—for all of us. The Pope points out the Jesus barely arrives in a town than he seeks out those in need of spiritual healing from the effects of sin and in need of mercy and forgiveness. It is also true that Pope Francis has not suspended or revoked a single principle of Catholic morality or doctrine (despite his many critics) while being perfectly clear that in pastoral outreach, God's mercy and forgiveness is the primary message, and on that basis the rest can be put into the proper perspective via vis mercy.

A recent book by Pope Francis' friend and consultant, Cardinal Walter Kasper, titled *Mercy: the Essence of the Gospel and the Key to Christian Life,* carefully reworks the history of Catholic theology weaving the title into every aspect of the Church and its self-understanding. Blazoned across the cover of his copy of this book the Pope wrote: 'This book has done me so much good. Francis.'

How can we make mercy the key to our life as a Christian? We might begin by never letting our favorite opinions, stances, ideologies, quirks of temperament block the power of God's mercy to meet the heart and mind of those we come into contact with every day. A good way to celebrate the gift of mercy is thru a reconversion to a spirituality of forgetfulness of self, so others see the mercy of God in our behavior.

The Misery of Sin

'If your hand causes you to sin, cut it off. It is better for you to enter into life maimed than with two hands to go into Gehenna, into the unquenchable fire.' (Words taken from the holy Gospel of St. Mark. (Mk. 9:43)

Hear how St. Catherine of Sienna advised her followers about cutting it off:

I long to see you so clothed in the garment of divine charity, in true and perfect love, that every other love will leave your heart and affection. For our soul cannot be clothed in two different loves at the same time. If our soul is clothed in the world, it cannot be clothed in God; the two are quite opposed to one another. When we set our love and affection on the world, we love ourselves with a sensual love. We are always seeking after honors, status and wealth; for pleasure, enjoyment and sensual comforts—pleasures that lead souls to eternal death. For those who love the world and its pleasures excessively are invariably rooted in pride, and from pride all the vices are born.

Oh what misery such hearts reap! They are totally immersed in perverse worldly concerns. The result is that they lose the life of grace and win death; they lose the light and enter the darkness. They fall into the vile servitude of sin, and so become servants and slaves of what is not. And a worse fate there could not be. Such souls literally take themselves and put themselves into their enemies' hands.

Now I don't want this for you… I want you with a true and holy diligence to strip your heart and affection of this perverse one and clothe it in love for Christ crucified, with perfect blazing charity, living always in love and affection for your neighbors. Such love is full of joy and gladness and is thoroughly pleasant. It fills and fattens the soul with virtue. It opens the eye of understanding and makes it gaze steadily upon Christ crucified and his indescribable love for us. So by loving we are filled with love and take to following in the footsteps of Christ, finding continual delight in virtue. We conform ourselves with him in difficult times by being patient. And when we are prospering, and enjoying worldly gratification and prestige and fame, we conform ourselves with him in our disdain for these things. That is, just as Christ disdained worldly pleasures, so we too disdain them with true and holy diligence when we are clothed in love.

The Month of May

'A great sign appeared in the sky, a woman clothed with the sun, with the moon under her feet, and on her head a crown of twelve stars.' (Words taken from the book of Revelation. (Rev. 12:1)

In prior years, May was when we always had a procession to crown the Virgin's statue. Ever wonder why the month of May is set aside to honor Mary? Maybe because May is mostly taken up with the weeks to celebrate the Resurrection. *Venerable Louis of Granada* a Spanish Dominican priest and a good friend of St. Charles Borromeo, prayed as follows:

'Now, Lord, you have glorified that holy flesh which suffered on the cross. But remember that your flesh is the flesh of your Mother and that she also suffered in seeing you suffer on the cross. She was crucified with you and therefore it is just that she should rise with you. It is the statement of your apostle, Paul, that those who were your companions in suffering should also be your companions in glory. And since this Lady was your faithful companion in all your sufferings from the crib to the cross, it is fitting that now she should share your joys and glory. Brighten that darkened sky, reveal that eclipsed moon, disperse the clouds of sorrow from her sorrowful soul, dry the tears of her virginal eyes, and command that the flowers of summer return after the winter of so many rains.'

Perhaps at that time the Blessed Mother was at prayer in her oratory, waiting for this new light to break forth. She cried forth in the interior of her soul and addressed herself to her beloved Son, now in the third day of his death: 'Arise, my glory; return, Victor, to the world. Gather your flock together, Good Shepherd. Hear, my Son, the cries of your afflicted Mother and since these sighs made you come from heaven to earth, let them now raise you from hell to earth.'

Saint Padre Pio expressed it this way:

'Oh, the lovely month of May! How well this month preaches the tenderness and beauty of Mary! When I think of the innumerable benefits received from the dear Mother of God, I am ashamed of myself, for I have never sufficiently appreciated her heart and her hand which have bestowed these benefits upon me with so much love, and what troubles me most is that I have not repaid the affectionate care of this Mother of ours as much as I should.'

'How often have I confided to this Mother the painful anxieties that troubled my heart! And how often has she consoled me! But many times, when my heart was at peace, I have forgotten my duty of gratitude toward this blessed heavenly Mother!'

'Poor dear Mother, how you love me! I observed it once more at the dawn of this beautiful month. What great care she took to accompany me to the altar this morning. It seemed to me that she had nothing else to think about except myself as she filled my whole heart with sentiments of holy love. I felt a mysterious fire in my heart which I could not understand. I felt the need to put ice on it, to quench this fire which was consuming me. I wish I had a voice strong enough to invite the sinners of the whole world to love Our Lady.'

Mother Teresa of Calcutta

'Then the king will say to those on his right, 'Come, you who are blessed by my Father. Inherit the kingdom prepared for you from the foundation of the world. For I was hungry and you gave me food, I was thirsty and you gave me drink, a stranger and you welcomed me, naked and you clothed me, ill and you cared for me, in prison and you visited me.'' (Words taken from the holy Gospel of St. Matthew. (Mt. 25:34-36)

As you know, *Saint Teresa of Calcutta* (+1997), was founder of the Missionaries of Charity and awardee of the Nobel Peace Prize; In her honor and because we can learn so much from her about loving Jesus, I would like to share a couple of thoughts about what love meant for her.

Someone asked Mother Teresa: 'You love people whom others consider the rejects of humanity. What is the secret that allows you to do this?' To which she replied:

'My secret is very simple: I pray. Through prayer I become one in love with Christ. I realize that praying to him is loving him. That means that I am fulfilling his commandment. Let's not forget what he tells us: *I was hungry and you fed me not.* The poor who live in the slums of the world are the suffering Christ. The Son of God loves and dies through them, and through them God shows me his true face. For me, prayer means being united to the will of God twenty-four hours a day, to live for him, through him and with him.'

Again they asked: 'If Jesus is head of the Church, shouldn't the Church show a different face and be more exemplary?' Mother Theresa's answer: 'But, who is the Church? You and I. Jesus doesn't need palaces. Only men need them. The Church are those who follow him. Following him is something that I try to do every day. We live surrounded by people who are hungry for love. That is what we need to give them. If everyone was capable of discovering the image of God in their neighbors, do you think that we would still need tanks and generals?'

The Mystery of Faith

'I am the bread of life; whoever comes to me will never hunger, and whoever believes in me will never thirst....(W)hoever eats this bread will live forever.' (Words taken from the holy Gospel of St. John. (Jn, 6: 35 and 51)

I acknowledge that my soul hungers and thirsts for God. I firmly believe that hunger and thirst are appeased by union with Jesus through faith. He recognized that by our very nature we seek a haven of rest. When He made the promise of living forever, He was speaking of such a place of rest. Only by accepting Jesus and His promises can we be assured of repose. He seemed to warn us of this condition by suggesting that without the necessary faith, people would not follow him. And as if to prove what he said, many of those who heard his Eucharistic exhortation did in fact leave Him because they lacked faith in Him. Without believing in Jesus as the way to everlasting life, how could they possibly believe one of the most difficult of all His doctrines, one which cannot be proven by anything visible, our Sacrament of Love!

When he spoke to His first followers, Jesus kept stressing the need for faith. It is still important in our day, that I value this virtue if I am true to believe in what the priest at Mass proclaims to be the mystery of faith. What is merely visible soon grows common and quickly fails to stir emotion. Any face, any scene, however beautiful, loses its stimulating power over us when we become used to it.

That is why the Blessed Sacrament never becomes common or usual. There is enough about it that is sensible for our human natural faculties to get a foothold, but the full grasp of it comes from my faith in Jesus. In the Eucharist, there is no human face, no human figure. But there is a presence, which obtains all of its power of stimulating my soul, all of its emotional control of me, from something much better than ordinary sight; namely, my spiritual faith in Jesus. In the Eucharist, there is only room for pure faith, because we have nothing to go by except the words of God, those memorable sentences that are the essence of the Mass: 'This is my body' and 'This is my blood.' The Eucharist is rightly called "the Mystery of faith".

I profess anew my faith in the Body of Christ. Jesus, my nourishment and my strength, I believe in you—help my unbelief.

The Mystery of Love

'I am the living bread that came down from heaven; whoever eats this bread will live forever; and the bread that I will give is my flesh for the life of the world.' (Words taken from the holy Gospel of St. John. (Jn. 6:51)

Listen to a paraphrase of what St. John Vianney, patron of priests, said about this verse of scripture:

If we consider all that God has made, heaven and earth, and that beautiful order which reigns in this vast universe—all manifests an infinite power which has created all things, an admirable wisdom which governs all things; and a supreme goodness which provides for all with the same facility as if it were occupied by one creature alone; all these marvels cannot but fill us with admiration and astonishment.

But if we speak of the adorable sacrament of the Eucharist, we may say that here is the marvel of the love of God for us. Here it is that his power, his grace and his goodness shine in a manner altogether extraordinary. Here is the bread come down from heaven, the bread of angels, which is given us for the food of our souls; here is the bread of strengthening which comforts and sweetens our sorrows, the traveler's bread, the key which opens heaven to us. 'He that receives me,' said the Savior, 'shall have eternal life.' And to give us this bread, Jesus multiplies miracles, turns the world of nature upside down, and suspends all it laws.

Nothing can be compared to the Eucharist. By baptism, it is true, we receive the title of God's children; heaven is opened to us as a consequence, and we are made participators in all the treasures of the church. By reconciliation, the wounds of our soul are healed, and the friendship of God is restored to us. By confirmation, Jesus Christ gives us the spirit of life and power. By the sacrament of the sick, he clothes us with the merits of his death and passion. By holy orders, he communicates to the priest all his powers. By matrimony, he sanctifies all our actions, even those in which man seems only to follow natural inclinations. All these are mercies truly worthy of a God who is in all things infinite!

But all this seems to be only an apprenticeship of his love for people: In the adorable sacrament of the Eucharist he goes further, He gives us himself;

It is Jesus prolonging his life and his benefits in our midst. O inestimable grace, immense, incomprehensible, divine liberality.

Pain of Loss

'…for if he were not expecting the fallen to rise again, it would have been useless and foolish to pray for them in death.' (Words taken from the second book of Maccabees. (2Mac. 12:44)

St. Paul taught 'it is a salutary thing to pray for the faithful departed.' In our time, we have All Souls Day and the whole month of November as a reminder to do this. And we have the scroll here to remind us to pray for the departed from our parish in the last twelve months. This is rooted in the church's strong conviction that we, the living, have a serious responsibility in charity to pray for those who have died, but who must yet complete the purification process every human needs to be able to enjoy the beatific vision, the vision of God.

A favorite prayer during the month of November from our funeral liturgy beseeches Our Lord: 'O gentlest heart of Jesus, ever present in the Blessed Sacrament, ever consumed with burning love for the poor captive souls in Purgatory, have mercy on them.' Very appropriate for us as we adore Jesus in the Eucharist this morning.

Thinking of the love that Jesus in the Blessed Sacrament has for the poor souls, we might ask ourselves, 'How strong is my love for them?' The Little Flower, St. Therese, used to offer the little things of her day so that Jesus would release one more soul from Purgatory.

We also should be praying for the people a departed soul leaves behind to grieve. I became one of those people with the death of my beloved wife a couple of months ago. Despite all the words of comfort and sympathy cards and Masses being offered for her soul, I learned there is such a thing as pain of loss.

Meditating on this, I thought of the Blessed Virgin. We remember what we call her seven sorrows—from the words about a sword piercing her heart, to the passion, death and placing of the Body of Jesus in the sepulcher. But I would suggest there is another sorrow, perhaps more painful of all. I refer to the pain of loss which Mary must have suffered for many years from the Ascension of Jesus to her own Assumption.

How Mary must have missed the comforting words of her divine Son! How she must have missed His presence in the company of their friends! How she must have missed His loving kiss! How she must have reviewed in her mind all the cures and works of mercy she had seen him perform!

November is also a month to remember our own mortality. To pray that we will have a happy after life. We don't like to think about death—or least our own. The older I get, I find myself, of necessity, thinking of my own demise, of when my name will be on this scroll. Mother Teresa once said, 'Death is the most decisive moment in human life. It is like our coronation: to die in peace with God.'

Peace and Joy

'I will go up the altar of God—To the God who gives joy to my youth.'

Thus did the priest and the altar boy begin the Holy Sacrifice of the Mass (in Latin of course) when I was such an altar boy years ago. Only sometime later did I come to appreciate the importance of God making me joyful as we approached that holy altar to renew his sacrifice on the Cross.

As a devout Catholic I learned that joy was one of the gifts of the Holy Spirit which should infuse every moment of my day. Joyfulness is one mark of those who follow Jesus, one that invites others to share in the peace and happiness that Our Lord wishes to animate in the souls of all.

Mother Teresa of Calcutta used to teach her nuns that their service to the poor and sick and marginalized should always begin with a warm smile. Why? Because the smile was an indicator of wishing to bring peace and joy to all. And who would turn down an offer to be happy even if it came from a complete stranger?

In our parishes today, every effort is made to greet newcomers with a warm smile of friendship, of kindness, of being welcome to worship with the family of their fellow parishioners. Often volunteers serve as official greeters at the doors of the church. In many cases, that is the first indication of what kind of parish this is. And as the old saying goes, 'You only get one time to make a first impression.'

At least, that is the intent. The problem is that today's parishes are mostly too big to let all get to know each other; too structured to permit only a small percentage to get to know more than a few faces around them; too busy with meetings, fund raising and similar impersonal activities which scare many to even try to develop friendships. Peace and joy do not seem to find a place on the parish calendar for too many.

Peace Be with You

'Peace, I leave with you; my peace I give to you…' (Words taken from the holy Gospel of St. John. (Jn 14:27)

One of the central themes of the Paschal season has to do with peace.

The following reflections come from the words of the late Archbishop Martinez, the first Primate of Mexico.

When the angels announced to the world, the incomparable joy of the birth of Jesus, they sang, 'Glory to God in the highest, and Peace to people of good will.' Both of these summarize the entire work of Jesus in this world, the very reason for His becoming man: to give glory to God and bring peace on earth. Peace is the gift that Jesus brought us from heaven, a gift so beautiful, so profound, so efficacious that we will truly never comprehend it. If we truly understood this God-given gift of peace, we could appreciate how it is the synthesis, the very climax, so to speak, of all the graces and heavenly blessings we have received from Jesus Christ.

Love is the seal of Christ. It is not just one of his many gifts; it is his singular gift. On that unforgettable night, the last that he spent on earth, the night of the gift of the Eucharist, Jesus left peace to his loved ones, saying: 'Peace is my bequest to you' (Jn 14:27). Then, after his resurrection, during the 40 days we commemorate in the Easter season, Our Lord's customary greeting to his apostles was this: 'Peace be upon you!' Furthermore, he recommended that in pursuing their apostolic mission, they should always say these same words upon arriving at any house: 'Peace be upon you!'

Holy Mother Church, the perpetuation of Jesus through the centuries, understands Our Lord's intention. By adopting her Master's expression in her liturgy, she constantly invokes peace upon her children. Almost all of the sacramental rites terminate with an expression of peace. The newly baptized, the Christian strengthened by confirmation, the sinner purified in the sacrament of reconciliation, all receive a message of peace: 'Peace be with you' or 'The Mass is ended. Go in peace.' Often during the sacrifice of the Mass, the priest wishes us, 'The peace of the Lord be with you' To which we respond, 'and with your spirit,' because Jesus said while importing peace to us, we are to give peace to one another.

Obviously, the peace spoken of is not just the absence of warfare or other hostile behavior—it is the calmness of knowing that we can place all our trust in Jesus.

Pentecost

'I will ask the Father, and he will give you another Advocate to be with you always, the Spirit of truth....' (Words taken Fromm the holy Gospel of St. John. (Jn. 14:16)

This Sunday we will great each other with a big Happy Birthday, as we celebrate the birth of our church born of the holy Spirit. Whenever we say the Apostles' Creed, we profess our belief in the Holy Spirit. But did you ever ask yourself what it is that you believe about Him?

Pope Benedict XVI said, 'The Holy Spirit has in some ways been the neglected person of the Blessed Trinity. Clear understanding of the Spirit seems beyond our reach.'

God the Father seems to be easily envisioned as the Creator and ruler of the universe. With the help of poets and artists, we make the Father into a semblance of someone's loving grandfather.

God the Son, because he shared our humanity is easy to picture as an infant who grew up to be an itinerant preacher and who ended up suffering a horrible passion and death as our Redeemer.

But the Holy Spirit? We tend to give up after drawing a picture of a dove, or by saying, 'No wonder we used to all Him the Holy Ghost.' It might help if we reflect on what the Spirit did and continues to do for us.

The Nicene Creed teaches us perhaps the most important gift of the Spirit. It says, 'I believe in one Lord, Jesus Christ who by the Holy Spirit was incarnate of the virgin Mary and became man.' The Spirit was the source of life of the God-man, Jesus. He is the source of our lives too, our first gift.

On Pentecost, we recall the words of Jesus that he "will send another advocate who will make clear to you everything I have taught you". So that is the gift we call understanding. The Spirit continues to do this through the words of Scripture which he authored, and by the inspirations he provides for all of us, which we call the gift of wisdom. At the time of his ascension, Jesus told his followers that the Spirit will provide the strength to carry out the mission he is giving them to convert the whole world. We call this the gift of fortitude.

There are so many other things the Spirit does for us. Let us be content with mentioning just one more. We are baptized by the Spirit and fire; and we receive him again in confirmation. Is he then through with us? No. Jesus spoke of the "indwelling" of the Spirit. Our dwelling is something permanent. When we go on vacation and stay in a hotel, we do not call that our dwelling.

When we rent a condo by the water so as to enjoy the beach, we do not call that our dwelling. When we seek shelter from an air raid, we do not call that our dwelling. When we go on a safari, we do not call that our dwelling.

So the Spirit dwells in us, takes up his home in us, resides within us on a permanent basis. And there he acts as a comforter. He is compassionate; he helps us through troublesome times; he gives the strength to carry our little crosses; he provides solace and peace and joy.

What does all this have to do with our adoration of Jesus on our altar? Jesus said the Spirit will be another advocate. Jesus was our first advocate, so whatever we learn about the Spirit must also be true about Jesus here on our altar. Studying the Spirit increases our knowledge of Jesus also.

As we celebrate the season of Pentecost, let us try to grow closer to the Spirit as the source of our life, our strength, our guide, our comforter.

As a little addendum to our reflection this morning, let me ask you on Fathers' Day to remember and adore the Father of us all, God the Father.

O my soul, bless God the Father;
All within me, bless his name:
Bless the Father and forget not
All his mercies to proclaim,
Who forgives your transgressions,
Your diseases all he heals;
Who redeems you from destruction,
Who with you so kindly deals.

Perseverance

'By your perseverance you will secure your lives.' (Words taken from the holy Gospel of St. Luke. (Lk. 21:19)

Jesus did not say by your fasting, or your solitude and silence, or by singing of psalms, although all of these are helpful in saving your soul. But he said by patient endurance in every trial that overtakes you. And in every affliction, whether this be insolent and contemptuous treatment, or any kind of disgrace, either small or great, whether it be bodily weakness, or the belligerent attacks of Satan or any trial whatsoever caused either by other people or by evil spirits.

By patient endurance, you will win life for yourselves. Although to this must be added wholehearted thanksgiving and prayer, and humility. For you must be ready to bless and praise your benefactor, God the Savior of the world, who disposes all things, good or otherwise, for your benefit. St. Paul writes: **'Let us...persevere in running the race that lies before us.'** (Heb 12:1). 'With patient endurance, we run the race of faith set before us.' For what has more power than virtue? What more firmness or strength than patient endurance? Endurance, that is, for God's sake. This is the queen of virtues, the foundation of virtue, a haven of tranquility. It is peace in time of war, calm in rough waters, safety amidst treachery and danger. It makes those who practice it stronger than steel. No weapons or brandished bow, no turbulent troops and advancing siege engines, no flying spears or arrows can shake it. Not even the devil himself standing by with all his armies and devices will have power to injure the man or woman who has acquired this virtue through Christ.

What does this look like in daily life?
To leave the stones unthrown,
To turn the other cheek,
To bear a load an extra mile,
To listen more than speak;

Such are the marks of love,
The testaments of grace,
The daily glimpses of the cross
Christ calls us to embrace

Praise the Lord

'Let us praise him the more, since we cannot fathom him, for greater is he than all his works; Awful indeed is the LORD's majesty, and wonderful is his power.' (Words taken from the book of Sirach. (Sir. 43:29–30)

Our service on First Fridays is called Exposition and Adoration of the Blessed Sacrament. What does it mean to adore Him? Venerable Mother Julienne Morrell, a Dominican nun who was the first woman to receive a Doctor of Laws degree, and who died way back in 1653, explained it thus:

We should be inspired by several motives. The first of these is the countless number of great and infinite benefits which we have received from the divine bounty, to which we owe praise and benediction with all our might in gratitude for the same, spending and consuming ourselves wholly in its service, rendering glory to it in heart and tongue, and with David inviting all that is within us to bless God's holy name. For, as St. Hilary declares, 'I owe to God primarily that all my strength and all my senses and my substance should proclaim his praises incessantly.' It is for this that we have received from God the body and its members, the soul and its powers; that out of all and with all we should honor and serve him.

The incomprehensible grandeur of the perfections of our God should also move us urgently to praise and glorify him. For his perfections are so infinitely great and his grandeurs so infinitely perfect, that all we might do is nothing compared to what is due to him. Should all the hairs of our head become tongues to praise him, should all the drops of our blood become inflamed hearts to love him, and were we to do naught else but perpetually praise him in love and love him in praise, even that would be nothing compared with his deserts.

And to this I would add the thought that what we aspire to is spending eternity in heaven doing nothing but rendering Him praise, and you begin to understand how important it is to sing the Lord's praises day and night and to practice that here before the Blessed Sacrament exposed on our altar or in the tabernacle.

Prayer

'Ask and it will be given to you; seek and you will find; knock and the door will be opened to you.' (Words taken from the holy Gospel of St. Matthew. (Mt.7:7)

Jesus then shows how much of a loving Father we have by asking, 'What father would give his son a stone when he asked for a loaf of bread, or a snake when he asked for a fish.' This analogy is used to set us at ease, to remind us that God says to us when we begin our prayer, 'Poor child, give me your heart.'

We know prayer should be a two-way conversation: first, listening to God, but sometimes we rush in and do all the talking. Other times we are hesitant because we realize we seem to be always asking for things. But don't we realize he pursues us with his undying love?

You give alms to a beggar on the street; you pray for an assassin to atone for his crime. Why? Probably because you know we are supposed to have love for everyone, which prompts our compassion. But are you asking for their love in return? If they offered their friendship, you would probably rebuff it.

The thing about prayer is that God treats us differently. No matter what the condition of our soul God still loves us and wants us to love him. Jesus told us, commanded us, to pray. Why? As our master, he is entitled to our homage. But he does not need our praise, he needs our love and that is what we show when we pray.

If you have children, you know how much they know you love them, so they do not hesitate to come to you with their needs. And you know you would do anything you can to satisfy them. So it is with our Father. If you have a close friend, you know what it is to share both good and bad. Shortly after my wife died, I was trying to organize things around the house. When I picked up our family bible, I found notes here and there in my wife's handwriting, dressed, 'Dear Jesus' and signed 'your friend, Pat.' By her prayer, my wife was that close to Jesus.

Purgatory

Eternal rest grant unto them, O Lord, and let perpetual light shine upon them. May their souls and the souls of all the faithful departed through the mercy of God, rest in peace. A traditional prayer for the departed.

In November, the Church invites us to pray for the souls of the faithful departed. The funeral liturgy of the Church is full of beautiful prayers of mercy, calling us to beg from God that he not look harshly upon the sins of the deceased, no matter how numerous or dark those sins may have been. These prayers remind us that God is much more merciful that we normally imagine.

Think about the wake service or funeral Mass that you have attended. We tend to think about the good aspects of the deceased person. And that is good, for we can be edified in some way by the life of just about anyone. But the reality is that we are all sinners, and the departed one we are extolling has probably sinned somewhere along the way, for as Jesus himself told us, 'The spirit is willing, but the flesh is weak.'

That being the case, our departed relative or friend may not have achieved the state of hotness which St. Paul tells us is necessary in order to see God. Such a soul is in need of repair. Sin distorts the soul, but God can straighten it out, as gold is purified in the furnace.

That brings us to the concept of Purgatory, a topic that is not spoken of from the altar very much. In some circles, it is considered gauche to admit that there is such a place or state as Purgatory. But Pope Benedict XVI wrote: 'I would go so far as to say that if there were no Purgatory, then we would have to invent it, for who would dare to say of himself that he was able to stand directly before the face of God? We do not want to be a pot that turned wrong, that has to be thrown away; we want to be able to be put right. Purgatory basically means that God can put the pieces back together again; that he can cleanse us in such a way that we are able to be with him.'

The Catechism of the Catholic Church reminds us that the souls of the faithful departed for whom we pray ardently are those who "die in God's grace and friendship, but who are still imperfectly purified; then after death they undergo purification, so as to achieve the holiness necessary to enter the joy of heaven". (CCC 11030)

Recognizing that it is the mercy of Jesus in the Eucharist which is at work in the purification process, let us humbly ask him in the Eucharist to remember his promise to His Father that He would not lose anyone sent to him, as we have all been.

The Real Presence

"Whoever eats my flesh and drinks my blood has eternal life, and I will raise him on the last day…This is the bread that came down from heaven. Unlike your ancestors who ate and still died, whoever eats this bread will live forever.' …Then many of his disciples who were listening said, 'This saying is hard; who can accept it?' …As a result of this many (of) his disciples returned to their former way of life and no longer accompanied him. Jesus then said to the Twelve, 'Do you also want to leave?' Simon Peter answered him, 'Master, to whom shall we go? You have the words of eternal life. We have come to believe and are convinced that you are the Holy One of God.' (Words taken from the holy Gospel of St. John. (Jn. 6:54…68)

Simon Peter, always speaking for the others, here acknowledges that Jesus is God, therefore to be believed literally when he explains about his real presence in the Bread he will give to his followers. At another time, when Jesus asked, 'Who am I,' it was Peter again who confessed his belief in Jesus as the Messiah, One therefore who was to be adored. Others had thought Jesus to be Johns the Baptist, or Elijah or one of the prophets. Those people were just that: people who did good for a time, but then died. They were not to be adored as Jesus was and is. So ask yourself as you contemplate him in the Eucharist. 'Who do you say Jesus is?'

Blessed John Henry Cardinal Newman, the English preacher, commented on these words of Jesus as follows: 'About these words I observe first, that they evidently declare on the face of them some very great mystery. How can they be otherwise taken? If they do not, they must be a figurative way of declaring something which is not mysterious, but plain and intelligible. But is it conceivable that he who is truth and love itself, should have used difficult words when plain words would do? Why should he have used words, the sole effect of which, in that case, would be to perplex, to startle us needlessly? Does his mercy delight in creating difficulties? Does he put stumbling blocks in our way without cause? Does he excite hopes, and then disappoint them? It is possible he may have some deep purpose in so doing, but which is more likely, that his meaning is beyond us, or his words beyond his meaning?'

All who read such awful words as those in question will be led by the first impression of them, either with the disciples to go back, as at a hard saying, or with Saint Peter to welcome what is promised: they will be excited in one way or the other, with incredulous surprise or with believing hope. And are the feelings of those opposite witnesses, discordant indeed, yet all of them deep, after all unfounded? Are they to go for nothing? Are they no token of our Savior's real meaning? This desire, and again this aversion, so naturally raised, are they without a real object, and the mere consequence of a general mistake on all hands, of what Christ meant as imagery, for literal truth? Surely this is very improbable.

Persons there are who explain our eating Christ's flesh and blood as meaning merely a pledge of the effects of Christ's passion of his body and blood. But how can Christ's be giving us his flesh and blood mean merely his giving us a pledge of his favor? Surely these words are too clear and precise to be thus carelessly treated. It increases the force of this consideration to observe that the manna to which he compares his gift, was not a figure of speech, but a something definite and particular, really given, really received.

The Real Presence 2

'What wonderful majesty! What stupendous condescension! O sublime humility! That the Lord of the whole universe, the Son of God, should humble himself like this under the form of a little bread, for our salvation.' These are the words of St. Francis of Assisi as they should be ours in front of Jesus on our altar.

Last week in the gospels Jesus took a couple of polls. He asked **'Who do people say that I am?'** (Mk. 8:27) And only Peter responded **'You are the Messiah.'** (Mk. 8:29

In recent months, two polls were conducted: one by the Pew Research firm and another by the Catholic Leadership Institute, asking Catholics if they believe that the bread and wine actually becomes the body and blood of Jesus in the Eucharist. In the Pew study, 45% of all Catholics said the Church teaches the bread and wine are only symbols. Of Catholics who attend Mass once a week only 63% know and accept the Church's teaching about the Real Presence. And for those who attend only monthly or once a year, 75% to 87% believe the Eucharist is just a symbol.

In the second study of a larger sample, of weekly Mass attendees 72% have it right; but that is less than ¾ths and most Catholics do not go to Mass every week, and they fall heavily into the symbol only group.

These numbers are not anything new. Most researchers have been calling our attention to this lack of faith for years. I myself, in my active consultant days, conducted surveys in a few parishes and it astonished the pastors to learn that only two-thirds of their parishioners believed in the true presence, which as you know is clearly stated by Jesus in St. John's gospel, chapter 6, the Bread of Life discourse.

Now you are here, attending Mass regularly, and professing your believe in the true presence, wishing to adore Jesus in the Eucharist. So why bother you with all these statistics? First of all, because you should know about this sad state of affairs. Also because we are our brother's keeper. And because just as we are called to help those whose physical health and well-being take a turn for the worse, so we should come to the aid of those whose spiritual life is weakening. And because, as soon to be beatified Archbishop Fulton J Sheen once said: 'If you do not behave as you believe, you will end up believing as you behave.'

In other words, since the presence of Jesus in the Eucharist is central to our faith as the one who motivates us to love our neighbor and care for those less well off than we are, any lessening of our belief in the Blessed Sacrament will lead to less actions of charity and not living our faith! Knowing and believing are indispensable, but the goal is Eucharistic living.

What to do about all this? Please forgive me if I seem to be preaching to the choir. Bear with me for just a few minutes more. Many are the reasons for the growing lack of true belief. Not enough is said about this from the altar. Not enough attention is paid to all the papal encyclicals and documents about the Eucharist. Too often it is just assumed that anyone who comes to Mass must hold strongly to the teachings of the Church. But for you and me: It has been said that our Catholic faith is not so much taught as caught. That means others will follow the example of what they see and accept as worthy of imitation. Those of us who cling to the truth of the Eucharist have a responsibility of showing that belief to others who may not be as strong in their belief. We can pray, we can continue to study, we can speak if the occasion presents itself; but most of all we can show by our reverence that we really believe this is our God under the appearance of a little piece of bread. And we can encourage daily Mass attendance which changes a believer from someone who fulfills a Sunday obligation to someone who treats the Eucharistic Lord with generous love.

Here are some ways we can help a doubter become a strong believer. First, we can cultivate a reverence in receiving. We can dress modestly and not come to Church straight from the beach in swimming attire. We can genuflect reverently before the tabernacle when we enter church and not just slide into the pew. We can spend time before Mass in private one-on-one conversation with Jesus who is already present in the tabernacle and not be a distraction to others by chatting and visiting with every new arrival in church, virtually ignoring Jesus' presence. (A warm welcome is one thing; a gab fest is something else.). We can approach the altar to receive Him with dignity, concentrating on whom we are to receive and not gaze around to see who else is in line. We can smile in answer to the Eucharistic minister's smile when actually receiving the Host in our hand or on our tongue, and not grab the Host as if it were a piece of candy. By paying attention to these things, we will be showing by example that we have not turned the post Vatican 11 changes in the way we receive communion into a total disregard for the solemnity of the Sacrament, and de-emphasizing Christ's true presence.

Thank you for reflecting with me on this—I am certain of your convictions about the Eucharist or you would not be here. But we are a community of faith, and it should bother us that so many of our fellow Catholics do not appreciate the wonder of the Sacrament of LOVE. And we can do something about it.

The Real Presence 3

'Then he took a cup, gave thanks, and said, 'Take this and share it among yourselves; for I tell you (that) from this time on I shall not drink of the fruit of the vine until the kingdom of God comes.' Then he took the bread, said the blessing, broke it, and gave it to them, saying, 'This is my body, which will be given for you; do this in memory of me.' And likewise the cup after they had eaten, saying, 'This cup is the new covenant in my blood, which will be shed for you.' (Words taken from the holy Gospel of St. Luke. (Lk. 22:17–20)

We all recognize these as the words of consecration at Mass.

When Pope Benedict declared a year of Faith, he encouraged us to read and pray over the words of Vatican II and the catechism of the Catholic Church. To this end, I offer as our reflection the following paragraphs from the section of the catechism dealing with the words of consecration which bring about the Sacramental Presence in the Eucharist. (CCC, Par 1178–81)

'The Catholic Church has always offered and still offers to the sacrament of the Eucharist the cult of adoration, not only during Mass, but also outside of it reserving the consecrated hosts with the utmost care, exposing them to the solemn veneration of the faithful, and carrying them in procession.'

'The tabernacle was first intended for the reservation of the Eucharist in a worthy place so that it could be brought to the sick and those absent, outside of Mass. As faith in the real presence of Christ in his Eucharist deepened, the Church became conscious of the meaning of silent adoration of the Lord present under the Eucharistic species.'

'It is highly fitting that Christ should have wanted to remain present to his Church in this unique way. Since Christ was about to take his departure from his own in his visible form, he wanted to give us his sacramental presence; since he was about to offer himself on the cross to save us, he wanted us to have the memorial of the love with which he loved us to the end, even to the giving of his life. In his Eucharistic presence, he remains mysteriously in our midst as the one who loved us and gave himself up for us, and he remains under the signs that express and communicate this love.'

As John Paul II wrote: 'The church and the world have a great need for Eucharistic worship. Jesus awaits us in this sacrament of love. Let us not refuse the time to go to meet him in adoration.'

Repent

'Repent, for the kingdom of heaven is at hand!' (Words taken from the holy Gospel of St. Matthew. (Mt 3:2)

At the conclusion of a world synod, Pope Francis reminded us: 'Christ is alive!' We need to keep reminding ourselves of this, because we can risk seeing Jesus Christ simply as a fine model from the distant past, as a memory, as someone who saved us 2 thousand years ago. But that would be of no use to us; it would leave us unchanged; it would not set us free. The one who fills us with his grace, the one who liberates us, transforms us, heals and consoles us is someone fully alive. He is the Christ risen from the dead, filled with supernatural life and energy, and robed in boundless light. ...Alive, he can be present in your life at every moment, to fill it with light and to take away all sorrow and solitude.'

The holy father here is talking to the synod members as Jesus talked to his apostles when commissioning them to go out to the world and convert everyone. Jesus said, 'I am with you always, to the end of the age.' (Mt 28:20). Even if all others depart, he will remain, as he promised. This is the power of his resurrection.

In the third luminous mystery of the rosary, offered by Pope St. John Paul 11 as a summary of the public ministry of Jesus, Our Lord repeated one refrain over and over. **'Repent, for the kingdom of heaven is at hand'** (Mt 4:17). He was telling them that HE was the kingdom, that he had been sent from the Father, that he was one with the Father and wished to make all one with him the same way. St. Mark's version of this message goes a step further, for he quotes Jesus as saying, 'The time is fulfilled, and the kingdom of God is at hand: repent ye, and believe the gospel.' But most who heard him did not understand him nor accept his message.

Kneeling before Jesus in the Eucharist, we hear him telling us the same message: 'Repent, change your ways, be converted. You can do it because I am here with you, flesh and blood, body and soul. Remember that conversion is a daily necessity. You receive me in the Blessed Sacrament precisely to gain the knowledge, the courage, the will to draw ever closer to me, to glory that I am very much alive in your midst and remain your personal savior. Do not just remember me as someone who went from town to town in Galilee preaching and doing good for the people of that time. No—I am very much alive and talking to you in the same way. The kingdom is at hand. I am the kingdom. You do not have to wait until you pass from this life to be with me. You are with me today, tomorrow and always.'

\`\`\`\`\`\`\`\`

The Risen Christ

'We shall be like him, for we shall see him as he is.' (Words taken from the first letter of St. John. (1 Jn. 3:2)

How often have you heard some version of the following: 'Well, as long as you're a good person, what does it really matter what you believe or how you worship God?' This is the remark of a person who has reduced everything in religion—art, liturgy, prayer, the sacraments, etc.—to morality or ethics.

Obviously right behavior is important, but if you had asked one of the Church Fathers or medieval masters what Christianity is ultimately all about, they would definitely not have said it's all about ethics. They probably would have said, 'The essence is deification, or becoming conformed to the divine nature.' An adage on the lips of the Church Fathers was, 'God became man so that man might become God.'

In our Mass, the central act of our religion, the priest prays: 'By the mystery of this water and wine may we come to share in the divinity of Christ.' We pray to be deified.

During the Easter season we are confronted by the risen Christ, We see him appearing miraculously to his followers, under the species of a human body, but glorified beyond our power to imagine. First to the Magdalene, **'Stop holding on to me'** (Jn. 20:17)— because I have not yet returned to my Father. And then later to Thomas, **'Put your finger here and see my hands, and bring your hand and put it into my side, and do not be unbelieving, but believe.'** (Jn.20:27)

Today we look at the Eucharist on our altar, or in the tabernacle, and see that same glorified Christ now under the species of bread. We know this is he of whom the Father said **'This is my chosen Son; listen to him.'** (Lk.9:35) And what did Jesus say? **'Be perfect, just as your heavenly Father is perfect.'** (Mt.5:48)

One Easter appearance which must have taken place (though we have no accounting of it in the scriptures) would have been the reconciliation of Jesus with Peter. Poor Peter—he repeatedly comes up short in the gospels: doubting when trying to walk on water, questioning on the mountain, sleeping in Gethsemane, denying in Jerusalem. Yet Jesus reminded him that he was a rock and gave him the keys to his new church. Peter then became deified and became like his Master in being crucified.

So, live a moral life, yes. But do so because of your faith in Jesus. This is our destiny—to be like Him when we see Him as He is—to be deified!

The Risen Christ 2

'... (and you yourself a sword will pierce) so that the thoughts of many hearts may be revealed.' (Words taken from the holy Gospel of St. Luke. (Lk. 2:35)

During this Paschal season between Easter Sunday and Ascension Thursday the liturgy will recount many appearances of the Risen Christ. There are a total of eleven mentioned in the New Testament. Some are lengthy appearances to the Apostles and the travelers to Emmaus, and some are one-word statements that Jesus appeared to St. Peter and St. James, for instance.

In this month of May, there is one other assumed appearance that I would like talk about today. I mean the appearance of the glorified Jesus to His Blessed Mother. There is no mention of this in the Gospels, so what makes us think it did take place? There is no discussion of this in the early Church, but reviewing the appearances that are in the Gospels, we become convinced that most of them were to alleviate the fear, the disappointment, the sorrow Jesus' followers were undergoing after Calvary.

Then, recognizing the depths of Mary's devotion to and shared suffering with Jesus, we ask ourselves, 'What about an appearance to His Mother to alleviate somewhat the unimaginable loss she felt for three days?' From at least the 11th or 12th century, there were many devotees of Mary who believed such an appearance took place. Among those who held this belief were At Anselm, St. Albert the Great, St. Ignatius Loyola, St. Teresa of Avila, A special devotion of the Franciscans from 1422 has been the Franciscan Crown. This is a seven-decade rosary honoring the seven joys of Mary, the sixth of which is a reflection on the appearance of Jesus to Mary after His resurrection.

In our own day, Pope St. John Paul 11 said, 'From the fact that the Gospels do not relate an apparition to the Blessed Virgin, one must not deduce that the Risen Christ did not appear to Mary...On the contrary it is legitimate to think that His Mother may really have been the first person to whom Jesus appeared.'

This is a matter of personal and private devotion, not a formal teaching of the Church.

Since we do not know any of the circumstances, we might imagine Mary was at prayer as she was before the appearance of Gabriel. Like us, she could not completely understand why Jesus had to suffer and die, especially as she held the warmth of His just deceased and broken body as she held it in her arms at the foot of the Cross.

We can imagine such a loving embrace of these two immaculate ones as the world has ever seen, giving thanks to a merciful Father, and renewing their commitment to do all that was ordained by the Father for us insignificant children. We can picture a solicitous Son wiping away the tears of sorrow from such a beautiful face to be replaced with copious tears of joy.

As in all of the appearances of the Risen Christ, there are lessons for us. If I could only share in the faith and trust Mary had for her Son. If I could only appreciate the need for pain and sorrow as a prelude to everlasting joy. If I could only surrender myself to the loving arms of Jesus in peace and joy during this Easter season.

The Rosary

Two groups of students were getting ready to play a football game. Each team formed a circle at their end of the field to say a prayer. One team prayed: 'Our Lady of Victories, pray for us.' Then they looked at the other team and added, 'Our Lady of Sorrows, pray for them!' Mary is honored by many titles. Our Lady of Sorrows is one, which is celebrated on Sept. 15th each year. But if you look at the litany of Loretto, you will not find Our Lady of Victories.

That title goes back to the war between the Ottoman Turks who were taking captive and also slaughtering Christians. They were now marching on Europe headed for Italy and the Papal States. Pope St. Pius V knew the Christian army was greatly outnumbered by the Turks and he asked every Christian to pray to Mary for help in the battle. Those prayers were heard, and the pope then coined the title Our Lady of Victories. But it is not in the litany now—it has been replaced with the title Our Lady of the Rosary.

October is the month dedicated to Mary and her rosary. So many of the saints prayed the rosary every day. St. Padre Pio was said to have prayed the rosary 13 times a day. St. Louis de Montfort, perhaps the greatest Marian devotee of all time explained we do this because Mary is "the safest, easiest, shortest and most perfect way" to Jesus and to sanctity.

Some have asked, 'Why not pray directly to Jesus without having to go through someone?' Have you ever tried to talk to, or get an appointment with an important and busy executive, politician, superstar, or some such? Often you can succeed only by going through some intermediary. But more to the point about Jesus and Mary, just remember that the rosary, all four sets of decades, is called a short New Testament, because they describe all the events in the life of Jesus and Mary from the Anunciation of the birth of Jesus, through his life, passion, death and resurrection to the crowning of Mary as our Queen mother.

There is a true story about a baby named Herman who was born in 1013 with a deformed leg and a damaged cleft palate. His parents did not want to raise a handicapped babe so they brought him to the gates of aa nearby monastery and left him there. The monks found the infant, took him inside and raised him. His deformed leg and his cleft palate became the butt of many jeers and taunts by other youths, and he learned to find comfort in his rosary. He eventually became a member that monastery. He had a life-long devotion to Mary and was the author of many of our most well-known hymns to Mary. Look in your hymnal for Salve Regina Mater, or Alma Redemptoris Mater…and you will see at the bottom of the page "Attributed to Herman Contractus"—Herman the Cripple, who is now Blessed Herman.

The Rosary 2

'The Rosary, precisely because it starts with Mary's own experience, is *an exquisitely contemplative prayer*. Without this contemplative dimension, it would lose its meaning, as Pope Paul VI clearly pointed out: 'Without contemplation, the Rosary is a body without a soul, and its recitation runs the risk of becoming a mechanical repetition of formulas, in violation of the admonition of Christ. (Words from the encyclical of Pope St. John Paul II entitled "The Rosary":

October is the month of Our Lady of the Rosary. In his encyclical Pope, John Paul II insisted that the Rosary, 'though clearly Marian in character, is at heart a Christocentric prayer. It has all the *depth of the Gospel message in its entirety*, of which it can be said to be a compendium. It is an echo of the prayer of Mary, her perennial *Magnificat* for the work of the redemptive Incarnation which began in her virginal womb. With the Rosary, the Christian people *sits at the school of Mary.'*

To help contemplation and remind us that all the mysteries concern Jesus as well as Mary, John Paul suggests that when we say the rosary, we should hold and look at the crucifix in one hand and the beads in the other.

The Holy Father went on to say, 'I believe, that to bring out fully the Christological depth of the Rosary it would be suitable to make an addition to the traditional pattern which could broaden it to include *the mysteries of Christ's public ministry between his Baptism and his Passion.*' He called these the Luminous mysteries, because Christ in His public ministry showed Himself to be the light of the world. Each of these mysteries is *a revelation of the Kingdom now present in the very person of Jesus.*

Of special import to us as we adore Jesus exposed in the sacrament of the altar or in the tabernacle is the fifth Mystery of Light, the institution of the Eucharist, in which Christ offers his body and blood as food under the signs of bread and wine, and testifies **"to the end"** his love for humanity (cf *Jn* 13:1), for whose salvation he will offer himself in sacrifice.

In these luminous mysteries, apart from the miracle at Cana, *the presence of Mary remains in the background.* The role she assumed at Cana in some way accompanies Christ throughout his ministry. and it becomes the great maternal counsel which Mary addresses to the Church of every age: **'Do whatever he tells you'** (*Jn* 2:5). This counsel is a fitting introduction to the words/ signs of Christ's public ministry and it forms the Marian foundation of all the "mysteries of light".

The Sacred Heart of Jesus

'If you know me, then you will also know my Father. From now on, you do know him and have seen him.' Philip said to him, 'Master, show us the Father, and that will be enough for us.' Jesus said to him, 'Have I been with you for so long a time and you still do not know me, Philip? Do you not believe that I am in the Father and the Father is in me?' (Words taken from the holy Gospel of St. John. (Jn.14:7–10)

Here is how Bishop Jacques Bossuet (18th century) explains this quote:

Let us join St. Philip in saying with all our heart **'Master, show us the Father, and that will be enough for us.'** (Jn. 14:8) He alone can fill our emptiness, satisfy our needs, make us content, and give us happiness.

Let us then empty our heart of all other things, for if the Father alone suffices, then we have no need for sensible goods, less for exterior wealth, and still less for the honor of men's good opinion. We do not even need this mortal life; how then can we need these things necessary to preserve it? We need only God. He alone suffices. Possessing him we are content.

How courageous are these words of St. Philip? To say them truthfully, we must also be able to say with the Apostles, 'W**e have given up everything and followed you.'** (Mt.19:27). At the least, we must leave everything by way of affection and desire; that is, by an invincible resolution to attach ourselves to nothing, to seek no support except in God alone. Happy are they who carry this desire to its limit, who make the final, lasting and perfect renunciation.

As we converse this morning with the Sacred Heart of Jesus on the altar or in the tabernacle, these words of Bishop Bossuet remind us of the familiar quote from St. Augustine, 'My heart is restless until it rests in thee.'

This morning we see the Sacred Heart of Jesus before us on the altar or in the tabernacle. But as he told Philip, **'Whoever has seen me has seen the Father.'** (Jn. 14:9). So as we gaze on the second Person of the Blessed Trinity, we are also seeing the first Person, for they are consubstantial and inseparable, along with the Holy Spirit. We have here then all that we need. Let us endeavor let go of any attachment to things of this world. Let us sweep our heart clean of every last vestige of selfishness and leave room therein only for our God, our creator, our redeemer, our sanctifier, the source of divine Mercy.

The Sacred Heart of Jesus 2

'Take my yoke upon you and learn from me, for I am meek and humble of heart.' (Words taken from the holy Gospel of St. Matthew. (Mt.11:29)

Without a doubt, the Sacred Heart of Jesus in our Eucharist contains all virtues: humility, meekness, patience, love. But they are so excellent, so divinely infused into indescribable harmony, that as we look at him with love, we sense a singular purity that runs the whole gamut of heroism, sincerity, delicacy, tenderness, pain. We sense a unique, heavenly impression. At times, it is sublime indignation or holy anger driving the sellers out of the temple with a whip; and at other times the sweetness of love with which Jesus looked at the young man desirous of obtaining eternal life.

Sometimes that impression is a deep sigh of distress, as St. John relates in the account of the raising of Lazarus; Other times it is the human tender weeping of the same account. On some occasions, one senses the glory of Tabor; and on others, the agony of Gethsemane; again, the majesty with which he calmed the tempests, or the humility with which he allowed himself to be tied by the executioners. Sometimes we feel the courage with which he opposed the hypocrites; at other times one perceives the delicate tenderness with which he allowed the beloved virginal disciple to rest upon his breast.

But always it is an analysis of virtue, unique and immutable. His lips have the same accent when he rebukes and when he blesses. His eyes have the same depth when they flash angrily as when they allow the tenderness of his soul to shine forth. The heart that suffers and the heart that loves is the same heart, the one that sends forth rays of glory at the Transfiguration and a sweat of blood in the Garden; the one that pardons and caresses, the one immolated, the one that promises heaven upon the cross and gives itself in the Eucharist. It is the same divine reality that is revealed to us and is hidden from us, without our even seeing it in its fulness, though it is never completely hidden from us. Were he to show himself to us such as he is, his beauty would slay us. Were he to hide himself from us completely, we would die from cold and darkness.

These are some of the thoughts that overwhelm us as we look upon Jesus on our altar, trying to learn of his meek and humble heart.

Taken from Servant of God *Archbishop Luis Maria Martinez* (+1956)

Sacrifices

A girl of eleven, asked to teach a child of four to "make a sacrifice", taught him to make the sign of the cross. Asked why this should be a sacrifice, she answered with supreme wisdom, 'Because for a little minute you give all of yourself to God.'

For a little minute, the child stops jumping and shouting, he stands still, puts his feet together, uses his hands and his mind and his voice for his sign of the cross. He is offering himself to give honor to God.

When we make sacrifice, it is always thus, we have to give up something, not because it is a bad thing—for more often it is a good thing—but the offering of ourselves is a complete offering, it means a whole attention, a whole concentration, a whole donation. In the Old Law, God asked for the sacrifice of the first fruits, the best lamb, the first of all the flocks. He did not accept Cain's sacrifice, because it was not the best. In the New Law, he still asks for the first lamb of the flock, the richest fruit of the tree; he asks for Jesus Christ.

'He Himself bears the mature fruit of true solid virtues. If you want patience, he is the bedrock of meekness, since not a murmur of complaint was heard from the Lamb. If you want humility, He is the bedrock of deep humility, since God stopped down to humanity, and the Word stooped to the shameful death of the cross. If you want charity, he is that charity—and even more, for it was the power of love and charity that kept him nailed fast to the cross.'

St. Catherine of Siena (+1380), Doctor of the church, Dominican, stigmatist and papal counselor.

Self-Surrender

Jesus said to them, 'I am the bread of life; whoever comes to me will never hunger, and whoever believes in me will never thirst.... Everything that the Father gives me will come to me, and I will not reject anyone who comes to me, because I came down from heaven not to do my own will but the will of the one who sent me. And this is the will of the one who sent me, that I should not lose anything of what he gave me, but that I should raise it (on) the last day.' (Words taken from the holy Gospel of St. John. (Jn. 6:35–39)

Clearly here Jesus is exhorting his followers to take advantage of the offer he is making: Follow me faithfully and I will give you eternal life. That is what he meant by not having hunger or thirst. He does not promise that in this life, but wishes us to think with him of an everlasting life in heaven where there is no such thing as hunger and thirst, nor any other of the plagues of this world like suffering and pain of any kind. His flesh and blood as food in this life will satisfy our needs forever.

What must we do on our part? Surrender ourselves to his leadership. I must give him in this life the absolute oblation of myself, surrendering all that I have to his sovereign will, in order that his will, without asking me for my opinion, may do with me what he wills.

In that way, my will lives in his. Like two streams that come together to form one river, like two drops that become just one, like two flames that become just one light, I want my will to become merged with his. Giving up my will to his is a total surrender of myself, because my will is the prime mover in my every thought, word or deed.

Jesus on our altar. I love you with your own will and thank you for the knowledge and gift of your divine will.

Seven Secrets of the Eucharist

For our reflection today, I offer the following summary of the book by Vinny Flynn entitled *The Seven Secrets of the Eucharist* in which he states that Pope St. John Paul II said these truths need to be rediscovered or rekindled.

First. The Eucharist is not Christ on the cross—it is Jesus NOW, enthroned in heaven. The loving God, the living Bread, living and glorious in the Eucharist we have is a real person, the flesh and blood of the Second Person of the Blessed Trinity.

Second. Christ is not alone. Christ is divine, and divinity equals Trinity. So, when we are in receipt of the Eucharist, or adore him on our altar or in Communion, we are receiving, praying to the Trinity. The three Persons cannot be separated. That means where Jesus is, so are the Father and the Holy Spirit. But there is more. Christ is a king, and do you know of a king traveling without a court? So when you adore the Eucharist, you are drawn closer to the court of heaven, including departed love ones, the saints, our Blessed Mother, and so on.

Third. There is only one Mass. The one Mass being offered by the high priest—Christ Jesus. The sacrificial Lamb. The paschal mystery is the one event that never stops. It transcends time. So in the Eucharist we are confronted by the death of Jesus on the Christ made present in this time and place.

Fourth. We have not just one miracle, but many. We have the transubstantiation, the Incarnation, the Trinity, our Redemption; we have the abyss of the mercy of God, deeper than the abyss of our sins.

Fifth. We don't just receive the Eucharist. We have transformed it and share in the divinity of Christ who humbled himself to share in our humanity.

Sixth. Every reception of the Eucharist is different from the last one and the next. We should become better at entering into the mystery of the Sacrament each time we go to Communion, otherwise it is just habit.

Seventh. There is no limit to how many times we can receive. We can receive him spiritually as often as we wish in a day. St. Maximilian Kolbe is said to have made a spiritual communion every 15 minutes. He prayed to Mary to help stay close to Jesus all day long/

Silence

'For it is written, 'Be holy because I (am) holy'' (Words taken from the first letter of St. Peter. (1Peter 1:16)

Jesus does not ask us to be wonder workers. All that is asked of us is to be more like Jesus—which is what holiness is—to grow in holiness a little bit day by day.

Mother Teresa reminded us that we were created to love and to be loved. And this is the beginning of prayer: to BE SILENT and acknowledge the love of God.

Jesus took Peter, Andrew and John up a high mountain to pray. Why there? Mainly because in that environment there would be no noise, no distractions, nothing but silence, to be broken by the voice of the Father. Omnipotent as He is, God does not wish to be competing against things of the earth for our attention.

In the book of Kings, we read about Elijah wishing to hear the voice of God. First there was a heavy wind storm, but the voice of God was not in the wind. Then there was an earthquake, but the voice of God was not in the earthquake. Then was a big fire, but the voice of God was not in the fire. Then there was the sound of utter silence, and he found God in a very small voice in the midst of that total silence.

On that mountain, the three apostles saw Moses and Elijah conversing with Jesus. What were they discussing? St. Luke tells us they were talking about the passion and death of Jesus which was about to take place. You will recall that both Moses and Elijah had suffered also. Elijah and Moses were witnessing the fulfillment of all that all the prophets had foretold about the Messiah. St. Elizabeth of the Trinity, a Carmelite nun, quoted a friend saying, 'We long to see the face of Jesus; faith is being face to face with God in the darkness.'

And so we pray often: Lord, make me holy. You sent your Son as an example and savior. Give us the grace to grow in Christ likeness. You have given us the example of saints throughout the ages, support us as we try to imitate them. You give us the Eucharist that we may enter into the mystery of your love; let us use the graces of all the sacraments to be more like you every day.

God is good, and getting better. (words suggested by the Letter from James, 1:1). That does not mean God changes from good to better. It means we get to understand the goodness of God a little better as we grow older and become more of an image of Jesus, our model. Holiness is union with God.

Christ must be present in every part of life if we are to be more and more like Him, our getting better.

Moses "saw" God in a burning bush on Mount Horeb. Years later, Elijah, wanting to pray about the unfaithfulness of the Israelites, went up Mt Horeb. He was told that there the Lord would pass by.

Prayer is the lifting and rising of our mind and heart to God. This is what we are doing here. Being here for adoration is our going up a mountain. There we wish to immerse ourselves in Jesus. That is like falling into a well, one that has no bottom. The deeper we go the more like Jesus we become. We will continue to fall because no matter how holy we become; we are not at the bottom yet.

We don't like silence; we like to be busy all the time; the hustle and bustle of daily living. Even in the midst of a conversation with friends, say over dinner, we become uncomfortable when there is silence, we go on saying anything because we feel awkward when there is silence.

For us, the many clamoring voices in our culture are trying to keep us from listening to the voice of good silence. St. James asks us to think about how we use our tongue, the source of our speech. Too often we use it to tear down people, when we are supposed to use it to praise God, to give comfort, to build up.

Silence 2

God achieves everything, acts in all circumstances, and brings about all our interior transformations. But he does it when we wait for him in recollection and silence. In silence, not in turmoil and noise does God enter into the innermost depths of our being.

God's presence has always been present in us in an absolute silence. And a human being's own silence allows him to enter into a relationship with the Word that is at the bottom of his heart. Man enters into a silence that is God.

Silence is not an absence. On the contrary, it is a manifestation of a presence, the most intense of all presences. The real questions of life are posed in silence. The greatest scientific discoveries are worked out in the quiet of a research lab. Our blood flows through our veins without making any noise; we can hear our heartbeat only in silence.

Man must stand or kneel or sit silently before God and tell him: God, since you gave me a desire for perfection, make me love you more and more. I surrender wordlessly to you, O Lord. I want to be docile and malleable like clay in your hands, for you are a skillful, benevolent potter.

Adapted from *Cardinal Robert Sarah*, Prefect of the Congregation for Divine Worship and the Discipline of the Sacraments;

Sin

'Have mercy on me, God, in your goodness;
in your abundant compassion blot out my offense.
Wash away all my guilt;
from my sin cleanse me.
For I know my offense;
my sin is always before me. …
Turn away your face from my sins;
Blot out all my guilt.' (Words taken from Psalm 51:3–5, 11)

This is the most popular of the penitential psalms, sung by David when he is confronted by Nathan after his affair with Bethsheba. For our reflection, consider what St. John Eudes (+1680) said about sin:

Being the principle, the exemplar, and the end of man and of all creatures, God wishes men to return to him as to their origin, to imitate him, to model their life and their actions on him as their exemplar, to follow him as their rule, to work toward him with all their strength, by every thought, word and action, as to their last end. To render him capable of doing this, God has given man a mind, a heart, and a will to know and love him, to imitate him, and to trend unceasingly to him as to his center. And in order that man may do so with joy and facility, God has enlightened his mind with the light of faith, has poured divine grace into his soul, and enkindled love in his heart.

But what has ungrateful man done? He has become separated from God and devoted his interests to self. Instead of employing his love for God, he has devoted it to himself and developed self-love. Instead of returning to God as to his principle, he has turned away from him. Instead of referring to God all the blessings of nature and grace, man appropriates them to himself, who is only nothingness. Instead of following God as his exemplar and his rule, he follows the rule of his passions. Instead of allowing himself to be led by the spirit of God, he desires no other guidance than that of his own inclination. Instead of rendering to God as to his end, taking his repose in him and doing everything for him, man wishes to tend wholly to himself and to do everything for self.

Who is God? God is he whose will, interest, pleasure and honor should be performed before every other will, interest, pleasure and honor. What does the sinner do? He prefers his own will, interest, pleasure and honor. Thus he usurps the place of God, makes a god of self, falls into self-adoration, and pays self the homage that belongs to God alone. This is the extreme iniquity of sin. This is what we have done every time and as often as we have sinned.

St. Joseph, Patron of
the Universal Church

'In the sixth month, the angel Gabriel was sent from God to a town of Galilee called Nazareth, to a virgin betrothed to a man named Joseph, of the house of David, and the virgin's name was Mary.' (Words taken from the holy Gospel of St. Luke. (Lk. 1:26–27)

On Dec. 8th, we celebrate the feast of the Immaculate Conception of the Blessed Virgin. On that day recently, we observed the fiftieth anniversary of the decree of Pope Pus IX in 1970, formally declaring Mary's husband, St. Joseph, to be Patron of the Universal Church. To celebrate this anniversary, I would like to suggest that St. Joseph is a great model for us as we adore Jesus in the Blessed Sacrament.

First, a little about the circumstances surrounding the decree honoring St. Joseph. As Pius IX put it, 'in these most troublesome times the Church is beset by enemies on every side, and is weighed down by calamities so heavy that ungodly men assert that the gates of hell have at length prevailed against her.'

To seek heavenly protection against these enemies of the universal Church, at least three petitions were submitted to Pope Pius IX requesting that St. Joseph be proclaimed Patron of the Universal Church, signed by 118 bishops. by 43 superiors general of various religious orders, and by 255 others, 38 cardinals among them, including the future Pope Leo XIII.

The Pope wrote: 'It is thus fitting and most worthy of Joseph's dignity that, in the same way he once kept unceasing holy watch over the family of Nazareth, so now does he protect and defend with his heavenly patronage the Church of Christ.'

Today the Church faces the same kind of persecution all over the world from godless men. And in our own country, with the Immaculate Heart as our beloved patroness, the Church's teachings about life and marriage and the practice of religion are ridiculed and undermined by selfish individuals and organizations, using specious arguments about what the American people want.

Let us turn to St. Joseph our universal patron. As we sit or kneel here before Jesus, think of how close He was to his step-father. Joseph not only saw, but abode with, and embraced with paternal affection, and kissed, yes, and most sedulously even nourished him whom we faithful receive as the Bread come down from Heaven, that we might obtain eternal life. We have the body and blood of Jesus for ten or fifteen minutes when we receive the Eucharist; we kneel and adore Him on our altar for 20 or 30 minutes periodically. But Joseph wrapped Jesus in his arms 24/7 for many years. We adore and thank and beseech Jesus for our needs, but Joseph provided everything His divine son needed. Can anyone (except for Mary) be closer to Jesus than St. Joseph? As we seek to deepen our personal relationship to Jesus on our altar, let us ask St. Joseph, Patron of the Universal Church, to be our inspiration.

St. Joseph 2

St. Joseph is the patron and protector of the dying and dead.

One day in the late 18th century, Servant of God Mother Maria Cecelia Baij, OSB received a visit from St. Joseph. He appeared in eminent glory seated on a lofty throne. He told Mother Maria that the holy family had chosen her to receive and record revelations of his life. We learn of St. Joseph's great sufferings during his last days and the merits he gained. He suffered real anxiety and stress due to his illness and his inability to assist Jesus in the workshop, helping to provide for his and Our Lady's needs. St. Joseph endured these trials with great fortitude and patience, abandoning all to the Father's Loving Providence.

St. Joseph greatly pleased God with his constant care for the dying through his life here on earth. In addition to his corporal works of mercy on their behalf, he also pleaded for their salvation in his daily prayers—a spiritual work of mercy. Because of his devotion to the dying, St. Joseph was appointed as their special mediator and patron. God further granted that St. Joseph would continue to manifest his love for and service to these dying souls until the end of time. The day before he died, St. Joseph attained the degree of holiness God predestined for him. In his dying hour, Our Blessed Lord said to St. Joseph: 'My father, rest in peace and in the grace of your eternal Father and mine. To the prophets and saints, who await thee in Limbo, bring the joyful news of the approach of their redemption.' St. Joseph died before Our Blessed Lord's public life began. Even though he lived in silence here on earth where little is recorded about his life, St. Joseph merited a most active eternity interceding for the living, the dying and the Holy Souls in Purgatory.

Let us invoke St. Joseph under the title of Comforter of the Afflicted this November for our beloved dead and for all the holy souls in Purgatory.

St. Joseph 3

'Joseph, son of David, do not be afraid to take Mary your wife into your home. For it is through the holy Spirit that this child has been conceived in her.' (Words taken from the holy Gospel of St. Matthew. (Mt.1:20)

The appearance of the Archangel Gabriel to St. Joseph as he slept is often called the Annunciation to Joseph, because of the similarity with Mary's Annunciation.

The angel began with each of them by telling them not to be afraid. What a mark of respect shown to each of them by a messenger from God. Then the angel shared with them God's plan for the redemption of mankind. How fortunate they were for God to reveal his greatest plans and get each of them to realize the great love the Lord has for us all.

The reaction of Joseph to this message was immediate and obedient. For Matthew says, **'When Joseph awoke, he did as the angel of the Lord had commanded him and took his wife into his home.'** (Mt.1:24). Joseph shows here how righteous a man he was. Putting aside his own plan for solving the problem of a pregnant fiancé (divorce) he put into action what God decided he should dc. His trust/faith in God was a mirror of Mary's who had simply said, 'Let it be done to me according to your word.'

The only difference in these two annunciations was the tenor of Gabriel's message. For Mary, the message was a request; she was being asked to be the mother of Jesus, which she immediately consented to. Joseph, however received his message as a command to be the foster-father of Jesus, an order which he obeyed without a hesitation.

As we kneel before Jesus on the Eucharist, we might ask ourselves, 'Do I have the same kind of trust in the Lord? Is my obedience to his commands carried out as readily as theirs?' Their participation in our salvation's history was a kind of "blind" obedience because there was nothing for them to see, to touch, to test. They had only a very strange occurrence to guide their spiritual growth. It is much the same for us before the Body and Blood of Jesus. We have nothing to see, to feel, to test, other than our faith in the love our Savior has for us, hidden as he is under the species of bread and wine.

O Mary and Joseph, help me to grow in the virtues of trust and obedience as you did.

St. Joseph as Priest

Some apologists like to point out that St. Joseph has quietly become the forgotten man. While it is wonderful that he was "The Silent Man" in his life and in scriptural accounts of the Holy Family in deference to Jesus and Mary, his important role in salvation history requires us to pay him the honor due him. For many years, and with the approval of several pontiffs, every Wednesday of the year is dedicated to St. Joseph. Popes have enriched with indulgences the devout practice of honoring him on that day. Some bishops and pastors say the votive Mass of St. Joseph each Wednesday. Some people are studying books like "The Life and Glories of St. Joseph", praising him as just, meaning practicing all virtues. Some make a retreat to honor St. Joseph, ending with a self-consecration to him.

In our diocese and in our parish, Wednesday is also a day of prayer for vocations to the priesthood or religious life. I find that honoring St. Joseph on the same day is providential. For I like to think of St. Joseph as the first priest in the Catholic Church.

Oh, I know the Apostles were the first ones ordained by Jesus at the last supper to consecrate bread and wine in memory of Him, and pass on the priesthood to their successors in the Church. But ask yourself: are not our priests first and foremost custodians of the body and blood of Christ? Do we not recall many holy priests who were martyred as they tried to protect the Eucharist from violent desecration? And what was the mission of St. Joseph if not to protect, safeguard and nurture that same body and blood?

Doctors of the Church teach us that St. Joseph in his early years was a member of a Jewish synagogue and one who practiced the law of Moses. After Mary, he was the closest to the divine and human natures of Jesus. This ranks him above all other humans who are ordained "another Christ" through holy orders.

We call him foster-father. But his is no second-rate paternity. He was chosen to take the place of God the father with respect to the Word made flesh, the humanity of Jesus. He therefore had the three chief prerogatives and attributes of any father: affection, care and authority. First, his affection for Jesus was as if a spark of the infinite love of the Eternal Father for His Son filled the heart of Joseph. Next, his solicitude and care for this divine Son were inexpressible, for no father ever did so much or endured so much for his children as did St. Joseph for Jesus. And finally, he had paternal authority which is why Jesus was always submissive and obedient to Joseph.

St. Joseph is the patron of workers, husband and fathers, but I call him also (the patron of priests.

Sufferings

'Amen, amen, I say to you, unless a grain of wheat falls to the ground and dies, it remains just a grain of wheat; but if it dies, it produces much fruit.' (Words taken from the holy Gospel of St. John. (Jn. 12:24)

I kneel before Jesus in the Eucharist. I tell him all my troubles: I tell Him of the pain and suffering that is attacking my aging body; I tell Him of the bad habits I am trying to overcome; I tell Him of the work I never seem to finish; I tell Him of the broken promises I made so often. I feel I am a broken vessel.

Then I realize this is supposed to be a two-way conversation, so I stop and listen to Jesus. 'I told my followers many parables,' he says. 'Stories about things in their everyday life, so they could understand my teaching. Remember the one about a grain of wheat?' he asks. Then with love, he tells me about being broken.

'The seed breaks to give us the wheat. The soil breaks to give us the crop. The sky breaks to give us the rain. The wheat breaks to give us the bread. The bread breaks to give us the feast. There was once an alabaster jar that broke to anoint my glory.'

He invites me to reflect on all this fracturing. Then he looks right through the cracks at me. He says it slowly, like he means it: 'My heart was broken open with a soldier's lance, and my love poured out for you. Never be afraid of being a broken thing.'

I understand it then, why Jesus and his priests through the ages take the bread and break it. Until it is broken, it cannot be shared with others. For good reason, we speak of breaking a wild horse so it can be useful to humans. Unless I am broken, I will remain wild and wrapped up in my selfishness, of no use to others. But I remember Jesus telling me: **'Come to me, all you who labor and are burdened, and I will give you rest...For my yoke is easy, and my burden light.'** (Mt.11:28, 30). How can I waste time thinking of myself especially in the Eastertide when the Risen Lord invites me to follow Him all the way to the glories of Heaven! This is the day the Lord has made. Let us rejoice in it and be glad! Alleluia is our song!

Sufferings 2

During the years of His public ministry we see Jesus going from town to town as he cured multitudes who were sick with various diseases. Mary, often called Health of the Sick, mirrored her Son's compassion for the sick, which is why other multitudes go to Lourdes and other holy places each year to beg for her intercession.

But why do Christians do this? Have we not been taught to accept the will of God even if it includes suffering? Let us ask Jesus who is anxious to speak to us from his place here in the Eucharist. Let us listen to what he taught us in scripture about sickness and disease.

Everywhere Jesus went he was besieged by the sick and infirm. Nowhere do the gospels record that he instructed people simply to bear the suffering assigned to them. In no case does he indicate that a person is asking for too much and should be content with a partial healing or no healing. He invariably treats illness as an evil to be overcome rather than a good to be embraced. Illness, after all, is a result of original sin.

Jesus does not always respond immediately to the demands of the needy crowds. It is also reasonable to infer that Jesus did not cure every sick person within reach. At the pool of Bethsaida, for example, there lay a multitude of invalids, blind, lame, paralyzed, but the gospel mentions his speaking to and curing only one lame man. Scripture does not say that the Lord will always heal in response to our prayer. Jesus often did ask for an admission of faith before effecting a cure.

There are also instances in which Jesus initially seems to refuse a request, but then in response to persistent faith does perform a miracle. However, the gospels record no instance in which a person asks for healing and is categorically refused. This evidence from Scripture ought to challenge some people's ideas about the Lord's will to heal. Have we too often accepted the idea that sickness should simply be embraced? Do we too easily assume that if a person is ill, God wants things to stay that way for good? Could our resignation to illness or infirmity even sometimes be a cloak for unbelief? Jesus instructs his followers not only to visit the sick but also to cure them. Not all who bathe in the waters of Lourdes are cured, but it is possible that the Lord desires to heal far more often than we think.

Jesus on our altar, Jesus Divine Physician, help us to persevere in our prayer to be released of pain and suffering while uttering your own words at Gethsemane: **'...but not what I will but what you will.'** (Mk. 14:36)

Taste of Eternity

'Everyone who listens to my Father and learns from him comes to me. Not that anyone has seen the Father except the one who is from God; he has seen the Father. Amen, amen, I say to you, whoever believes has eternal life. I am the bread of life. Your ancestors ate the manna in the desert, but they died; this is the bread that comes down from heaven so that one may eat it and not die. I am the living bread that came down from heaven; whoever eats this bread will live forever; and the bread that I will give is my Flesh for the life of the world.' (Words taken from the holy Gospel of St. John. (Jn. 6:45–51)

Today let me paraphrase an exhortation of Pope Saint John Paul II:

The Eucharist is a straining toward the goal, a foretaste of the fulness of joy promised by Christ. It is in some way the anticipation of heaven, a "pledge of future glory" according to St. Thomas Aquinas. In the Eucharist, everything speaks of confident waiting "in joyful hope for the coming of our Savior, Jesus Christ". Those who feed on Christ in the Eucharist need not wait until the hereafter to receive eternal life; they already possess it on earth, as the first fruits of a future fulness which will embrace man in his totality. For in the Eucharist, we also receive the pledge of our bodily resurrection at the end of the world: **'For this is the will of my Father, that everyone who sees the Son and believes in him may have eternal life, and I shall raise him (on) the last day.'** (Jn. 6:40)

This pledge of the future resurrection comes from the fact that the flesh of the Son of Man, given as food, is his body in its glorious state after the Resurrection. With the Eucharist we digest, as it were, the "secret" of the Resurrection. For this reason, Saint Ignatius of Antioch rightly defined the Eucharist as "a medicine of immortality, an antidote to death".

This foretaste of heaven, kindled by the Eucharist, expresses and reinforces our communion with the Church in heaven. It is not by chance that both Eastern and Latin Eucharistic prayers honor Mary, the ever-virgin Mother of Jesus Christ our Lord and God, the angels, the holy Apostles, the glorious martyrs and all the saints. This is an aspect of the Eucharist which merits greater attention: in celebrating the sacrifice of the Lamb, we are united to the heavenly liturgy and become part of that great multitude which cries out: 'Salvation belongs to our God who sits upon the throne, and to the Lamb' (Rev. 7:10). The Eucharist is truly a glimpse of heaven appearing on earth. It is a glorious ray of the heavenly Jerusalem which pierces the clouds of our history and lights up our journey.

Vocations

'I am the good shepherd. A good shepherd lays down his life for the sheep...I am the good shepherd, and I know mine and mine know me.' (Words taken from the holy Gospel of St. John. (Jn.10:11 and 14)

Jesus also says to us: **'The harvest is abundant but the laborers are few; so ask the master of the harvest to send out laborers for his harvest.'** (Words taken from the holy Gospel of St. Matthew. (Mt. 9:37–38)

It is impossible to exaggerate the close relationship between the Holy Eucharist and vocations to the priesthood and the religious life. This is only to be expected once we realize that every vocation is a special grace from God, and the greatest source of grace that we have is the Eucharist.

Faith tells us that Christ is really present on our altars, that he really offers himself in the Mass, and we really receive his body and blood in Holy Communion. In every vocation, the living Christ is inspiring men and women to give themselves to him with all their hearts and follow him in the extension of his kingdom.

The Eucharist, therefore, is the best way to foster vocations. This means that persons who attend Mass, receive Communion and invoke Christ in the Blessed Sacrament obtain light and strength that no one else has. This enables us to appreciate the meaning of a vocation, and perhaps recognize one in someone we know, if not in ourselves.

Recognizing that without priests we can have no Eucharist, those of us who are really devoted to the Eucharist will pray hard that Jesus seed forth laborers to his harvest by fostering vocations.

Jesus exposed on the altar before me, or hidden in the tabernacle, issues a call to worthy men to follow you in offering the sacrifice of yourself on our altars.

The Way

'In my Father's house there are many dwelling places. If there were not, would I have told you that I am going to prepare a place for you? And if I go and prepare a place for you, I will come back again and take you to myself, so that where I am you also may be. Where (I) am going you know the way.' Thomas said to him, 'Master, we do not know where you are going; how can we know the way?' Jesus said to him, 'I am the way and the truth and the life. No one comes to the Father except through me.'' (Words taken from the holy Gospel of St. John. (Jn. 14:2–6)

For our reflection today, please listen to how St. Catherine of Sienna describes following Jesus as the Way:

Follow the standard of the most holy cross courageously and with blazing desire; follow in his footsteps along the way of suffering and of crucified loving desires. For the son or daughter should always be glad to follow his or her father, and the bride her bridegroom, so that if our father or bridegroom is in pain, we conform ourselves with him in pain, and if he is joyful, we conform ourselves to him in joy. Thus the Apostle Paul, that man in love, said of himself: 'I rejoice with those who rejoice, and I weep with those who weep.'

This is how we act if we are living in perfect charity, and by so doing we realize in ourselves what the Apostle Paul said: that those who share in the suffering, the cross of Christ, will also share in the consolation, will be in glory with Christ. Justly will God give them his inheritance, since for love they have left behind the inheritance and concerns of the world, have given up worldly pleasures and consolation and followed the cross of Christ crucified. They have embraced pain and disgrace and dishonor for love of him.

This is the fire in which your souls must burn with enflamed and loving desires. In nothing else must you take pleasure, for every other way is dark and obscure for us and leads to eternal death. So don't be careless. Be conscientious on this lovely straight way, Christ Jesus. Don't let selfish love or inattentiveness take control of you, because this is what keeps us from running, so that we stall along the way and keep turning back to look at what we have already plowed.

I urge you then for love of Christ crucified. because our good and gentle Jesus is so noble and generous—let us delay no longer. Let's keep in mind how short our time is. Let's redeem with holy sorrow and grief the time we have spent carelessly or lost, and in this way, we shall regain the past.

Who Am I?

'But who do you say that I am?' (Words taken from the holy Gospel of St. Luke. (Lk. 9: 20)

During a beatification ceremony in 1998 Pope Saint John Paul 11 offered the following reflection on this phrase:

'Jesus asked this question of his disciples one day as they were walking together. He also puts the same question to Christians on the paths of our time. As it was 2000 years ago in an obscure part of the then known world, so today human opinions about Jesus are divided. Some attribute to him the gift of prophetic speech. Others consider him an extraordinary personality, an idol that attracts people. Others believe he is even capable of ushering in a new era.'

'The question cannot be given a neutral answer. It requires taking of sides and involves everyone. Today Christ is asking: 'You Christians of this century, you citizens, who do you say that I am?' It is a question that comes from the heart of Jesus. He who opens his own heart wants the person before him not to answer with his mind alone. The question that comes from Jesus' heart must move our own: 'Who am I for you? What do I mean for you? Do you really know me? Are you, my witness? Do you love me?'

'Down the centuries there has been a continual struggle for the correct profession of faith. Thanks be to Peter, whose words have become the norm, **'You are the Messiah, the Son of the living God.'** (Mt. 16:16) These words should be used to measure the Church's efforts in getting to express in time what Christ means to her. In fact, it is not enough to profess with one's lips alone. Knowledge of scripture and tradition is important, the study of the catechism is valuable, but what good is all this if faith lacks deeds?'

'Professing Christ calls for following Christ. The correct profession of faith must be accompanied by a correct product of life. Orthodoxy requires orthopraxis. From the start, Jesus never concealed this demanding faith from his disciples. Actually, Peter had barely made his extraordinary profession of faith when he and the other disciples immediately heard Christ clarify what the Master was expecting of them: **'If anyone would come after me, let him deny himself, take up his cross daily and follow me.'** (Lk. 9:23). As it was in the beginning so it is today. Jesus does not look only for people to acclaim him. He looks for people to follow him.

Why Be a Christian?

Peter began to say to him (Jesus), 'We have given up everything and followed you.' (Words taken from the holy Gospel of St. Mark (Mk.10:28)

Notice that this reading says "Peter BEGAN" to say to Jesus. Apparently, he was not permitted to continue because Jesus saw he was as much as saying "what's in it for me". We can identify with St. Peter if we have ever felt tired of try to lead a good life and then are tempted to wonder if it's worth it all. And who hasn't at one time or other?

Jesus answered Peter by promising a hundred-fold return for a righteous life, both now and in the next life. I'd like to dwell a little on the now part. What does a hundred-fold look like while we are still alive? Some will find that reward in terms of prestige, power, possessions or other temporal good because Jesus does often give such worldly goods to those who love him. But most of us will find our earthly reward in the shape of peace of mind and the ability to accept the will of God.

Let me explain. If we face reality every person, Christian or non-Christian, will know that sooner or later he will have to give up everything: his loves, his possessions, even himself when death approaches. Sooner or later everyone has to do this. In the interim, every person will have his or her share of sickness, disappointment, loss of loved ones and other forms of trouble. We all will have crosses to bear. The advantage of being a Christian is that for us there is a meaning to those crosses. For us, the certainty of these crosses is accompanied by the promise of a resurrection. This is what Jesus meant when he said that those who love him will enjoy heaven on earth.

It's the story of Lazarus and the sick man all over again, The rich Lazarus found out that he was not ready to lose everything upon his death and suffered for it. Whereas the sick man at his feet was as happy as Lazarus because he knew his cross was going to end and he was preparing for that. He was already receiving recompense for accepting his lot in life.

So why am I a Christian? Because I have Jesus and my faith in him to accept my cross in preparation for a glorious resurrection.

You, Follow Me

'**When Peter saw him (John), he said to Jesus, 'Lord, what about him?'**
Jesus said to him, 'What if I want him to remain until I come? What
concern is it of yours? You follow me.'' (Words taken from the holy Gospel
of St. John. (Jn.21:21–22)

This interchange between Jesus and Peter is recorded at the very end of the
Gospel according to St. John. Jesus has just asked Peter, 'Do you love me?'
three times to give Peter a chance to undo his threefold earlier denial of Jesus.
Being satisfied with Peter's answers, Jesus said to him, 'Feed my sheep'
confirming Peter as the first pope responsible for leading and caring for the
church.

Peter then looks around and asks about John and is told very abruptly,
'What business is that of yours? You, follow me.' The messages is clear: do
not be worried about extraneous things; your only duty is to follow me. Forget
about other things; drop other concerns; you, follow me! I wonder if Peter
reflected on the time three years earlier when Jesus walked along the sea shore
and said to Peter, 'Follow me,' at which point Peter did drop everything else
and followed Jesus.

Today we look around as Peter did and are concerned about a lot of things:
wars, inflation, shortages, political divisions, personal crosses of every kind,
even disunity in the church, and the list goes on and on. As we look at Jesus
on our altar and ask him about all these things, He simply says, 'You, follow
me.' Does that mean literally to forget about those things? No, we should pray
about them, but leave them up to Jesus, following the example of Mary at Cana.

'**You, follow me;** Is Jesus talking only to Peter? Only to clergy and
religious? Or is he talking to you and me as we kneel or sit before him on our
altar this morning, '**You, follow me**'? How do we do that? He wants us to
listen to Him, to read about his teaching in scripture, to not only have faith in
Him but to practice our faith, to follow His example in coping with the crosses

we bear. That is the way we can contribute to the solution to all the problems we see around us, as well as our own. We are dealing with them only in as much as they bring us closer to the one, we follow, to give ourselves more and more each day to Jesus.

'You, follow me.' For how long? For now and forever. If we follow Jesus to the end of our life, we will also follow Him to heaven. He brought our humanity to the right hand of the Father and when doing so prepared a place for us by his side. How can we not thank Him for being the Way, the Truth and the Life?

'You, follow me!'